Researching the Polity:

A Handbook of Scope and Methods

Workbook

Second Edition

Laurence F. Jones
Edward C. Olson
Angelo State University

Cincinnati, OH
www.atomicdog.com

When ordering this title, use ISBN 1-59260-124-3
To order the online version (Online Study Guide Edition) of this title, use ISBN 1-59260-125-1

ISBN 1-59260-123-5

Library of Congress Control Number: 2004107872

Printed in the United States of America by Atomic Dog Publishing, 1148 Main Street, Third Floor, Cincinnati, OH 45202.

10 9 8 7 6 5 4 3 2 1

Researching the Polity:

A Handbook of Scope and Methods

Workbook

Contents

Chapter 7

Chapter 8

Chapter 9

Chapter 10

Preface

Researching the Polity: A Handbook of Scope and Methods, authored by Laurence F. Jones and Edward C. Olson, includes several chapters that introduce you to the topics political scientists study (the scope of political science). There are also chapters that inform you about the ways political scientists go about studying these topics (the methods of political science).

You will use this workbook with the Jones and Olson textbook referenced above. The workbook begins with an introduction to the basics of SPSS for Windows (SPSSW). SPSSW is a popular and comprehensive statistical analysis software system that allows you to store data, perform data transformations and analyses, and produce charts and graphs to display your results.

Chapters 2 through 4 explain how to use SPSSW to perform the basic statistical analyses presented in the textbook. Specifically, Chapter 2 covers univariate statistics, Chapter 3 discusses bivariate statistics, and Chapter 4 deals with multivariate statistics. Each chapter also includes exercises designed to enhance your understanding.

Chapters 5 through 9 cover the scope of political science. Specifically, an overview of the political world (Chapter 5), American politics (Chapter 6), public administration and public policy (Chapter 7), comparative politics (Chapter 8), and international relations (Chapter 9), receive attention. Each chapter includes research examples and exercises that will require you to use several *real* data sets to analyze the questions posed throughout the textbook and to complete the exercises in this workbook.

Chapter 10 covers the essentials of data entry. You will learn how to code data, create a new SPSSW data file, and enter data that pertains to America's ten largest cities. You will also learn how to save the data file you created.

You will be working with several real data sets when completing the workbook exercises. To work with the data set files, you must first download the files from the online Resources page for this workbook. The Resources page may be accessed by clicking the online Resources link in your Backpack. You will have the option of downloading the files to a floppy disk or your hard drive.

Make sure you keep your diskette in a safe place. You will need it so that you can analyze data associated with the questions posed throughout the textbook and to complete the exercises in this workbook.

Refer to Workbook Section 1-2f about SPSSW Guides for instructions on how to access one of the data files from your data diskette.

Print Edition and Online Study Guide Edition

Researching the Polity: A Handbook of Scope and Methods—Workbook, is available online as well as in print. The Online Study Guide Edition chapters demonstrate how the interactive media components of the text enhance presentation and understanding. For example,

- Highlighting capabilities allow you to emphasize main ideas. You can also add personal notes in the margin.
- The search function allows you to quickly locate discussions of specific topics throughout the text.

You may choose to use just the Online Study Guide Edition, or both the online and print versions together. This gives you the flexibility to choose which combination of resources works best for you. To assist those who use the online and print versions together, the primary heads and subheads in each chapter are numbered the same. For example, the first primary head in Chapter 1 is labeled 1-1, the second primary head in this chapter is labeled 1-2, and so on. The subheads build from the designation of their corresponding primary head: 1-1a, 1-1b, etc. This numbering system is designed to make moving between the Online Study Guide Edition and the print book as seamless as possible.

Chapter

Chapter 1

Getting Started

Key Terms

Data Editor window
Data View option
dialog box
output screen
SPSSW
SPSSW Guides
SPSSW menu bar
SPSSW title bar
Variable View option

Outline

1-1 Introduction

Welcome to the realm of political science research. This workbook contains exercises that will give you the chance to analyze key issues dealing with the several political science subfields covered in *Researching the Polity: A Handbook of Scope and Methods.* Each exercise requires you to analyze data from the data files furnished with the text. The exercises are designed to be used with SPSS for Windows (SPSSW). The data files allow you to examine survey data (The National Opinion Research Center General Social Survey) and political institutions such as the U.S. Congress, the Office of the President, the U.S. Supreme Court, the states, and nations of the world. The appendix at the end of this workbook describes each data file and cites the sources used to create each file.

1-2 The Basics of SPSSW

SPSS for Windows is a comprehensive integrated software system that allows you to store data, perform data transformations and analyses, and produce charts and graphs to display your results. **SPSSW** is a very popular statistical analysis package. More than likely, computer center personnel or your instructor has installed SPSSW on the computers in your school's computer labs.

SPSSW: A powerful statistical package that allows you to quickly generate decision-making information involving statistics. The program also enables you to understand and effectively present your results with tabular and graphical output.

Similar to other Windows-based programs, all functions in SPSSW involve the use of basic Windows elements such as drop-down menus, dialog boxes, and toolbars. The following section will introduce you to the basics of SPSS Windows.

Note: SPSSW, similar to most software programs, has a tutorial feature. Thus if you need help understanding the directions presented throughout this workbook, simply click on *Help* near the top right of the screen then select *Tutorial* (Figure 1-1).

1-2a Starting SPSSW from a Network

Your instructor or computer lab technician will probably help you get started, though you will likely find it pretty simple. To start the program you need to find

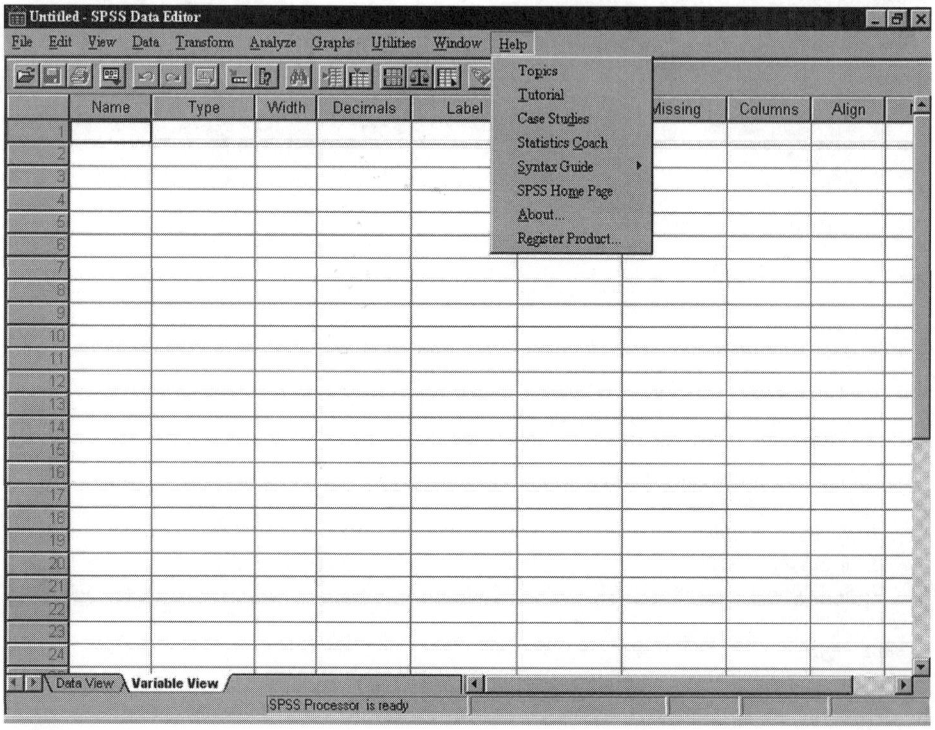

Figure 1-1
SPSSW Help and Tutorial Functions

the SPSSW icon. The icon should be found on the desktop or in a folder that contains other data analysis software programs. The icon is displayed in Figure 1-2. Start the program by double clicking with the left mouse button on the SPSSW icon.

SPSSW

Figure 1-2
SPSSW Icon

1-2b The SPSSW Data Editor Window

When you enter the latest versions of SPSSW, the SPSSW **Data Editor window** (Figure 1-3) is the first image you will see. The Data Editor is a spreadsheet that allows you to define variables and enter values. All of your data entry is done in this window. Notice that a dialog box is superimposed on the screen. This is the *What would you like to do?* dialog box. This dialog box is similar to other dialog boxes you will encounter when working with SPSSW. As you can see, you are presented with several options: *Run the tutorial; Type in data; Run an existing query; Create new query using Database Capture Wizard;* and *Open an existing file.* To complete the exercises in this workbook you will work exclusively with the *Type in data* and *Open an existing file* options. You can clear the dialog box by clicking on the X button in the upper right corner, or on the Cancel button at the bottom of the dialog box.

Data Editor window: The SPSSW window that contains the data in a spreadsheet format. This is the window used to run most commands.

1-2c The SPSSW Title Bar

The **SPSSW title bar** shows the name of the application, SPSS, and the window that is currently open. If you are entering data for the first time and have not saved the data as a file, the title bar displays the name of the file as *Untitled.* On the end of the title bar are common elements of Windows applications such as minimize and maximize buttons.

SPSSW title bar: The title bar shows the name of the application, SPSS, and the window that is currently open. If you are entering data for the first time and have not saved the data as a file, the title bar displays the name of the file as *Untitled.*

1-2d The SPSSW Menu Bar

The **SPSSW menu bar** appears below the title bar. The menu bar is the starting point for every task you will do in the SPSSW program. You use your mouse

SPSSW menu bar: The menu bar appears below the title bar. The menu bar is the starting point for every task you will do in the SPSSW program.

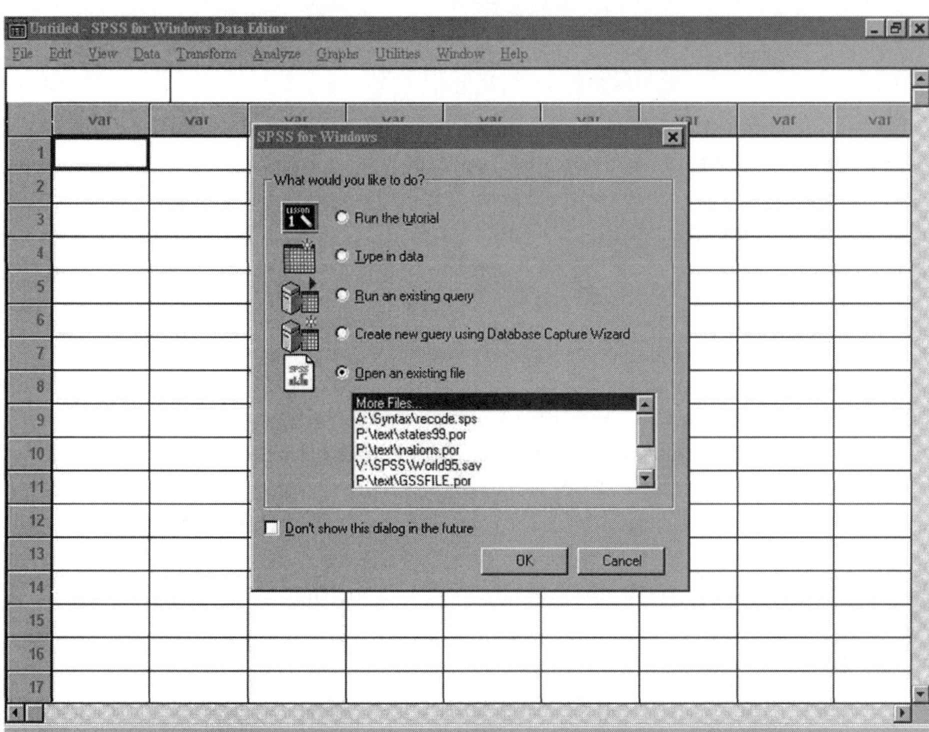

Figure 1-3
SPSSW Data Editor Window

Table 1-1 SPSSW Menu Bar Options

Option	Description
File	This option allows you to use the File menu. With this menu you can open and save data files and import spreadsheet and data files created by other software programs such as SAS and MicroCase. You can also print the Data Editor contents and the results of your analyses. Toward the bottom of the menu is the Recently Used Data option. This option provides a list of the most recent data files you have accessed. You can open these files by pointing to the file name and clicking your mouse.
Edit	This option allows you to use the *Edit* menu. With this menu you can perform many of the editing functions common to word-processing software such as Microsoft Word. You can, for example, undo entries; cut, copy, and paste data values; find data values; and change the way the variables in your data files are presented. You do this by using Options.
View	This option allows you to use the *View* menu. With this menu you can view or turn off status and toolbars. You also have the capability to change the print font and turn off the grid lines in the Data Editor. Lastly, you can control the way value labels and data values are displayed.
Data	This option allows you to use the *Data* menu. With this menu you can define variables and dates. You can also make global changes to a data file. You can, for example, transpose variables and cases, create subsets of cases to analyze, and merge several files. You can also split files and apply weights to cases.
Transform	This option allows you to use the *Transform* menu. With this menu you can use options such as *Compute, Count,* and *Recode* to make new variables.
Analyze	This option allows you to use the *Analyze* menu. With this menu you can perform numerous statistical analysis tasks. You can, for example, create reports; perform univariate, bivariate, and multivariate analyses; and determine the reliability of scales.
Graphs	This option allows you to use the *Graphs* menu. With this menu you can create bar and pie charts, scatter plots, and histograms.
Utilities	This option allows you to use the *Utilities* menu. With this menu you can get information about variables in the data file you are working with. You can also define a list of variables to appear in the dialog boxes.
Window	This option allows you to use the *Window* menu. With this menu you can switch between SPSSW windows and minimize the open windows.
Help	This option allows you to use the *Help* menu. With this menu you can access online help and run tutorials on the SPSSW applications and features.

Source: Adapted from Stangor, Charles, *Using SPSS 9.0 for Windows* (Boston: Houghton Mifflin Company, 2000).

cursor to point at the selection you want. Click once on a word in the menu bar to open the associated menu. From the associated menu you can select a command. For example, clicking once on the *File* menu and once on the *Open* command, will allow you to open an existing data set. Table 1-1 presents a brief description of the menu bar options.

Data View option: A viewing option that appears in the Data Editor window. The Data View option is the default option. This option displays the data values for each variable in a data set.

Variable View option: A viewing option that appears in the Data Editor window. The option presents information that describes each variable such as the type of variable (string, numeric), variable labels, and level of measurement for a particular variable.

SPSSW Guides: Guides that give you the essential information needed to complete a workbook task. Each line of the SPSSW Guide is an instruction intended to help you in completing an exercise.

1-2e The SPSSW View Options

Two view options appear on tabs at the bottom left of the Data Editor window: the **Data View option** and the **Variable View option** (see Figure 1-1). The Data View option, which is the default, presents the data values for each variable in a data set. When you click on the Variable View tab, you will see information that describes each variable. You will see, for example, the type of variable (string, numeric), variable labels, and level of measurement for a particular variable. Click on the Data View tab to return to the view that depicts the data values.

1-2f SPSSW Guides

Throughout this workbook, **SPSSW Guides** give you the essential information you need to complete each task. For example,

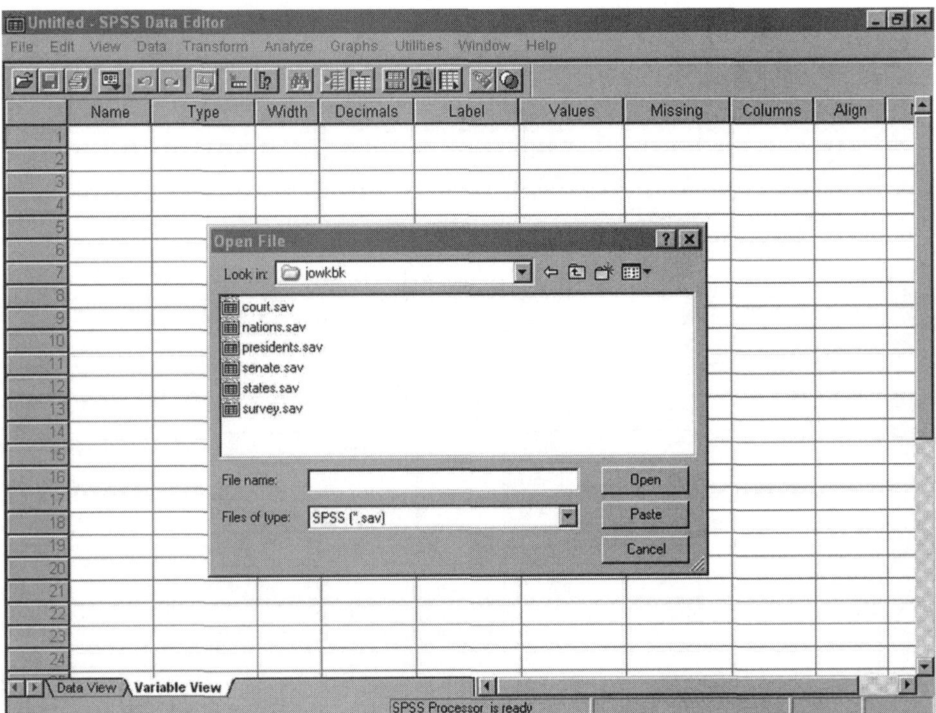

Figure 1-4
Open File Dialog Box

→ Data File: **PRESIDENTS**
→ Task: **ANALYZE—DESCRIPTIVE STATISTICS—FREQUENCIES**
→ Variable: **PARTY**
→ View: **FREQUENCIES**

Each line of the SPSSW Guide is an instruction intended to help you in completing the exercises. The following sections discuss in detail each step that is necessary to perform the above analysis example.

1. ***Open a Data File.*** Before you can do anything in SPSSW, you must open a data file. To open a data file, insert your data diskette in the computer's disk drive. Then click on the *File* menu and select *Open* then select *Data.* This action produces the Open File **dialog box** (Figure 1-4). Next, you need to click on the arrow for the *Look in* drop-down box located at the top of the Open File dialog box and select drive A. This produces the list of files presented in Figure 1-4.

   Click on the *presidents* file (or highlight the file and click on the Open button). After a few seconds SPSSW will open the file (Figure 1-5).

   The *Presidents* data file contains 43 cases (individual presidents) and 61 variables (characteristics of each case, for example, the name of the presidents). The rows represent individual presidents and the columns represent individual presidential characteristics. There are 43 rows and 61 columns. You can easily look at the various presidents and variables by using the appropriate scroll arrows at the top right, bottom right, or bottom left side of the Data Editor window. You can also use the arrow keys on the computer's keyboard. You can always see the data file that is currently open by looking at the file name shown in the title bar.

dialog box: An SPSSW window that allows you to enter information to run a command such as analyzing frequencies or producing a pie chart.

2. ***Selecting a Task.*** Once you have opened the data file you want to work with, you need to select a program task. To select a task, click on the *Analyze* option on the menu bar. There are several analysis tasks available for your use. For the exercises in this workbook, however, you will only be working with the following tasks: *Descriptive Statistics, Correlate,* and *Regression.* To complete

Figure 1-5
Presidents Data File

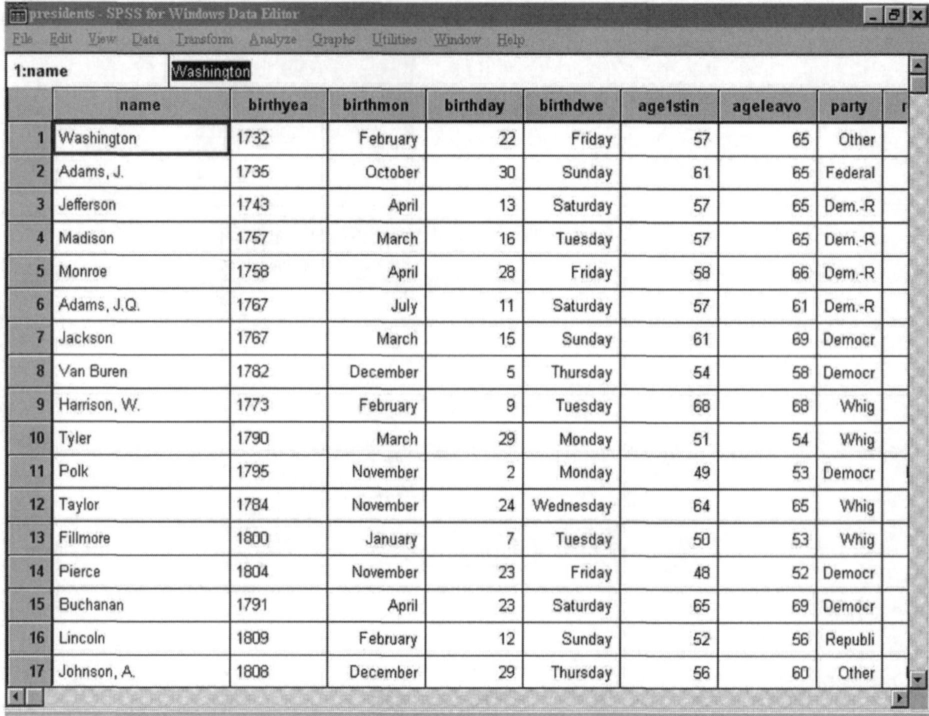

presidents - SPSS for Windows Data Editor

File Edit View Data Transform Analyze Graphs Utilities Window Help

1:name Washington

	name	birthyea	birthmon	birthday	birthdwe	age1stin	ageleavo	party
1	Washington	1732	February	22	Friday	57	65	Other
2	Adams, J.	1735	October	30	Sunday	61	65	Federal
3	Jefferson	1743	April	13	Saturday	57	65	Dem.-R
4	Madison	1757	March	16	Tuesday	57	65	Dem.-R
5	Monroe	1758	April	28	Friday	58	66	Dem.-R
6	Adams, J.Q.	1767	July	11	Saturday	57	61	Dem.-R
7	Jackson	1767	March	15	Sunday	61	69	Democr
8	Van Buren	1782	December	5	Thursday	54	58	Democr
9	Harrison, W.	1773	February	9	Tuesday	68	68	Whig
10	Tyler	1790	March	29	Monday	51	54	Whig
11	Polk	1795	November	2	Monday	49	53	Democr
12	Taylor	1784	November	24	Wednesday	64	65	Whig
13	Fillmore	1800	January	7	Tuesday	50	53	Whig
14	Pierce	1804	November	23	Friday	48	52	Democr
15	Buchanan	1791	April	23	Saturday	65	69	Democr
16	Lincoln	1809	February	12	Sunday	52	56	Republi
17	Johnson, A.	1808	December	29	Thursday	56	60	Other

the SPSSW Guide example, click on *Descriptive Statistics* to open its associated menu. Then click on *Frequencies* (Figure 1-6).

3. ***Selecting a Variable.*** Clicking on the *Frequencies* command will produce a list of the variables in the open data file (Figure 1-7). Note that the first variable (*name*) is highlighted. To obtain a description of a variable, you need to highlight and click on the variable with the right mouse button.

   Next, click on the *Variable Information* option. This will produce a dialog box similar to Figure 1-8. This dialog box provides a description of the

Figure 1-6
Frequencies Command

presidents - SPSS for Windows Data Editor

File Edit View Data Transform Analyze Graphs Utilities Window Help

1:name Washingto

Reports
Descriptive Statistics
Compare Means
General Linear Model
Correlate
Regression
Classify
Data Reduction
Scale
Nonparametric Tests
Multiple Response

Frequencies...
Descriptives...
Explore...
Crosstabs...

	name				thdwe	age1stin	ageleavo	party
1	Washington	1			Friday	57	65	Other
2	Adams, J.	1			Sunday	61	65	Federal
3	Jefferson	1		13	Saturday	57	65	Dem.-R
4	Madison	1		16	Tuesday	57	65	Dem.-R
5	Monroe	1		28	Friday	58	66	Dem.-R
6	Adams, J.Q.	1		11	Saturday	57	61	Dem.-R
7	Jackson	1767	March	15	Sunday	61	69	Democr
8	Van Buren	1782	December	5	Thursday	54	58	Democr
9	Harrison, W.	1773	February	9	Tuesday	68	68	Whig
10	Tyler	1790	March	29	Monday	51	54	Whig
11	Polk	1795	November	2	Monday	49	53	Democr
12	Taylor	1784	November	24	Wednesday	64	65	Whig
13	Fillmore	1800	January	7	Tuesday	50	53	Whig
14	Pierce	1804	November	23	Friday	48	52	Democr
15	Buchanan	1791	April	23	Saturday	65	69	Democr
16	Lincoln	1809	February	12	Sunday	52	56	Republi
17	Johnson, A.	1808	December	29	Thursday	56	60	Other

presidents - SPSS for Windows Data Editor
File Edit View Data Transform Analyze Graphs Utilities Window Help
1:name Washington

	name	birthyea	birthmon	birthday	birthdwe	age1stin	ageleavo	party
1	Washington	1732	February	22	Friday	57	65	Other
2	Adar				Sunday	61	65	Federal
3	Jeffe				turday	57	65	Dem.-R
4	Madi				uesday	57	65	Dem.-R
5	Monr				Friday	58	66	Dem.-R
6	Adar				turday	57	61	Dem.-R
7	Jack				Sunday	61	69	Democr
8	Van				ursday	54	58	Democr
9	Harri				uesday	68	68	Whig
10	Tyler				Monday	51	54	Whig
11	Polk	1795	November	2	Monday	49	53	Democr
12	Taylor	1784	November	24	Wednesday	64	65	Whig
13	Fillmore	1800	January	7	Tuesday	50	53	Whig
14	Pierce	1804	November	23	Friday	48	52	Democr
15	Buchanan	1791	April	23	Saturday	65	69	Democr
16	Lincoln	1809	February	12	Sunday	52	56	Republi
17	Johnson, A.	1808	December	29	Thursday	56	60	Other

Frequencies
name
birthyea
birthmon
birthday
birthdwe
age1stin
ageleavo
party
Variable(s):
OK
Paste
Reset
Cancel
Help
Display frequency tables
Statistics... Charts... Format...

Figure 1-7
Variables List

variable, the level of measurement for the variable, and the value labels for the variable.

You can move the highlight through the variable list several ways. First, you can use the up and down keys on your keyboard. Second, you can use the Page Up and Page Down keys to move through the list. Last, you can use the scroll bar located on the right side of the variable list window.

There are two ways to select a variable from the list for analysis. After highlighting the variable you want to analyze (for example, *party*), you can double click on the variable with the left mouse button. Or, you can click on

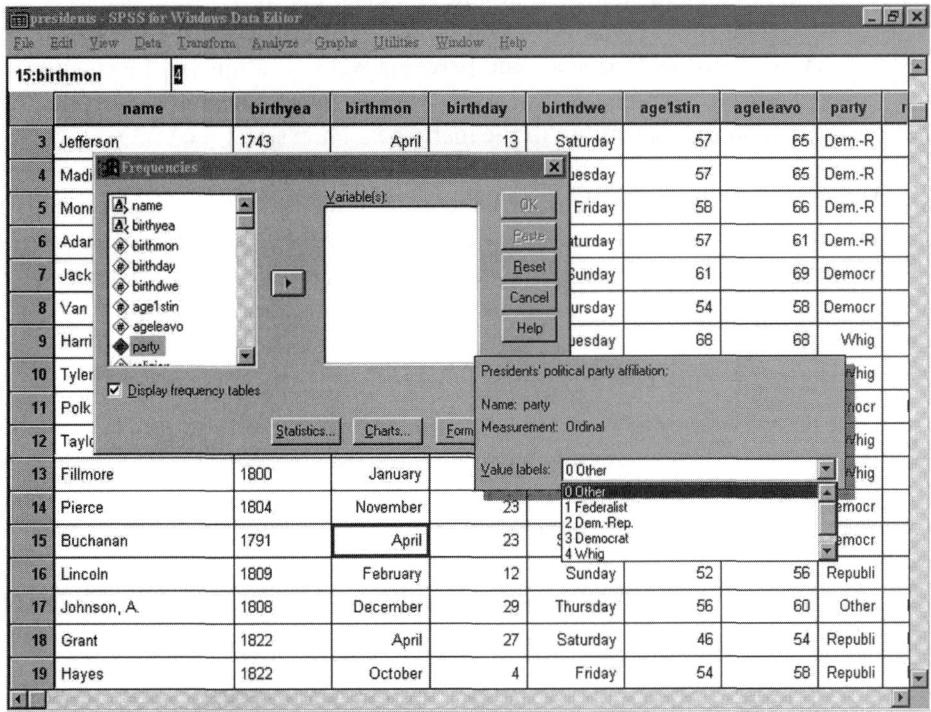

Figure 1-8
Viewing a Variable

Figure 1-9
Variable Selection

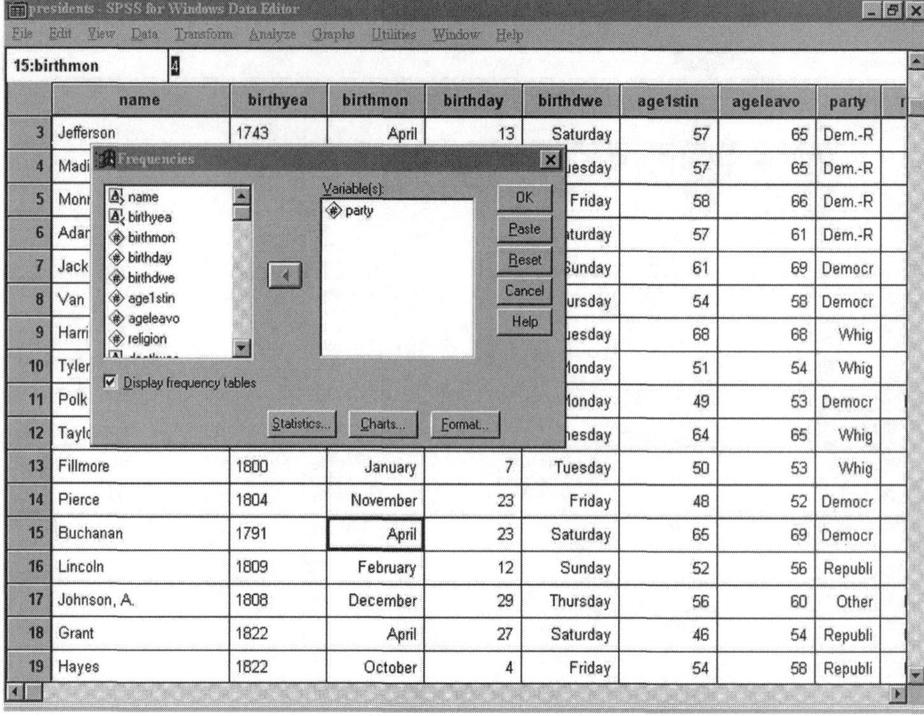

the arrow button. Note that once you have selected a variable (*party*), it is moved to the Variable(s) box to the right (Figure 1-9). You can select several variables at one time by pressing and holding the Control key on your keyboard while clicking on the different variables you wish to select. If you want to remove a variable from the Variable(s) box, highlight the variable then click on the arrow button.

As you can see, there are several buttons (Statistics, Charts, Format) at the bottom of the dialog box. We will explain the use of these buttons in Chapter 2.

output screen: The SPSSW window that contains the results of an analysis. The left side of the window summarizes the results in an outline. The right side of the window contains the actual results.

4. ***Selecting a View.*** To analyze a variable (for example, *party*) you need to click on the OK button. This action will produce an **output screen** (Figure 1-10) that shows statistics, frequency and percentage distributions, and the valid and cumulative percentages. There are two ways to exit the output screen. First, click on the *File* option in the menu bar. Then select the *Close* command. Or you can click on the X button at the top right of the window. When using either option, you will be prompted to save the output. If you want to save the output, you will need to identify the appropriate drive (*a:* or *c:*, for example) and directory to which you will save the output. When you close the output screen, you will return to the Data Editor window.

1-2g Saving a Data File

Saving a data file in SPSSW is a relatively simple procedure. If you have made changes to one of the data files included with the workbook such as the *presidents* file, you need to click on the *File* option in the menu bar and then click on the *Save* command. If you have created a new data file, you will also need to type the name of the file in the box at the top of the *Save File* dialog box.

As with any type of computer software, if you are making extensive changes to a file, you need to periodically save your work. You also want to take care that you do not write over an existing file. Thus, you may want to create a new data file with a new name (for example, *presidents1.sav*). To do this, click on the *File* option on

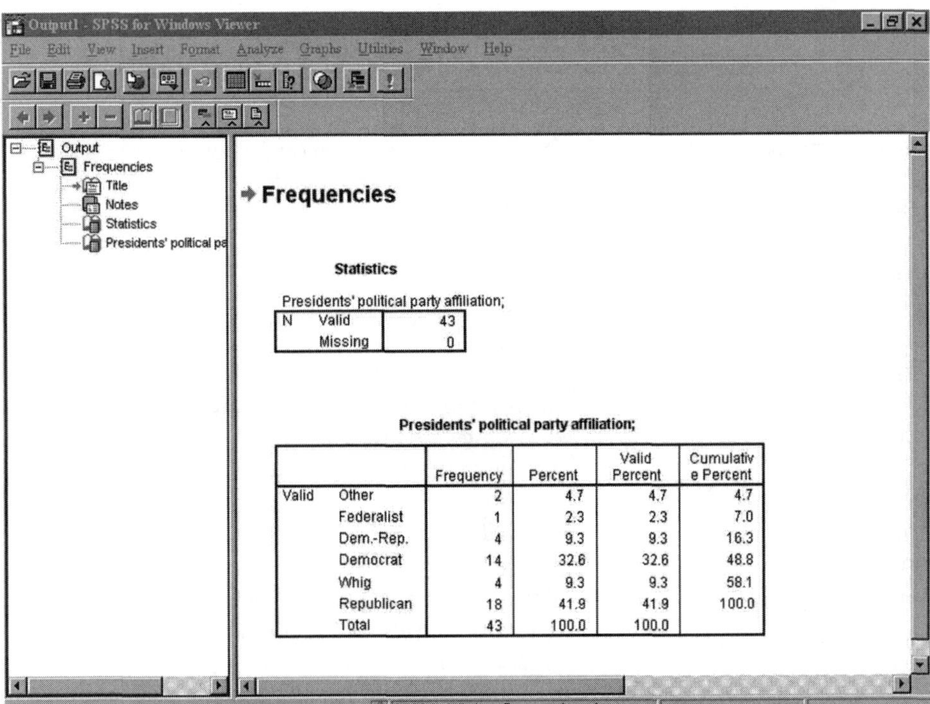

Figure 1-10
Output Screen

the menu bar and then select the *Save As* command. Select the drive to which you want to save the new file. Last, type the new file name in the *Save Data As* dialog box. To save a modified file, simply select the Save command on the *File* menu.

1-2h Exiting from SPSSW

When you finish your work in SPSSW, you must properly exit the program. All you need to do is click on the *File* option on the menu bar and then select the *Exit* command. Remember to save your work before you exit (if you forget SPSSW will warn you that you are about to exit without saving changes you made to the file). Also, do not forget to remove your data file diskette from the computer's external drive.

Exercises

Open the *presidents.sav* file and answer the following questions.

1. What does the variable **AGE1STIN** measure?

2. What is the name of the variable that measures the number of times a president used the pocket veto?

Open the *courts.sav* file and answer the following questions.

3. What does the variable **CHIEF** measure?

4. What is the name of the variable that measures the political party affiliation of a justice?

Open the *states.sav* file and answer the following questions.

5. What does the variable **PARKREV** measure?

6. What is the name of the variable that measures the infant mortality rate in a state?

Open the *nations.sav* file and answer the following questions.

7. What is the name of the variable that measures the maternal mortality rate for 1990?

8. What does the variable **LIFEXMAL** measure?

Chapter Quiz

1. When working in SPSSW, you can clear the dialog box by
   a. clicking on the X button in the upper right corner of the window.
   b. clicking on the Cancel button at the bottom of the dialog box.
   c. turning off the computer.
   d. You can clear the dialog box by performing either the actions in *a* or *b*.
2. When working in SPSSW, the title bar shows
   a. the name of the application.
   b. the type of graph you are analyzing.
   c. the window that is currently open.
   d. The title bar shows both *a* and *c*.
3. The SPSSW ___ is the starting point for every task you will do in the SPSSW program.
   a. title bar
   b. menu bar
   c. data view bar
   d. options bar
4. If you are entering data for the first time and have not saved the data as a file, the title bar displays the name of the file as ___.
   a. *to be titled*
   b. *titled.sav*
   c. *Untitled*
   d. **.sav*
5. When you click on the Variable View option, you will see
   a. the type of variable (string, numeric).
   b. variable labels.
   c. the level of measurement for a particular variable.
   d. each of the above.
6. With the ___ menu you can use options such as the *Compute, Count,* and *Recode* options to make new variables.
   a. *Transform*
   b. *Data*
   c. *Analyze*
   d. *View*
7. With the ___ menu you have the capability to change the print font and control the way value labels and data values are displayed.
   a. *Transform*
   b. *Data*
   c. *Analyze*
   d. *View*
8. With the ___ menu you can define variables and dates. You can also make global changes to a data file.
   a. *Transform*
   b. *Data*
   c. *Analyze*
   d. *View*
9. With the ___ menu you can switch between SPSSW windows and minimize open windows.
   a. *Transform*
   b. *Data*
   c. *Window*
   d. *Utilities*
10. With the ___ menu you can determine the reliability of scales.
    a. *Transform*
    b. *Data*
    c. *Analyze*
    d. *View*

Chapter 2

Univariate Statistics

Outline

2-1 Introduction

The purpose of this workbook chapter is to help you understand the basics of univariate statistics. Before you start working on the exercises in this chapter you should have a thorough understanding of Chapter 13 in the textbook.

Political scientists use univariate statistics to summarize data. Univariate statistics help you gain an understanding of the variables in a data set. In this chapter you will analyze frequency and percentage distributions, produce several charts, and interpret measures of central tendency and dispersion.

2-2 Frequency Distributions

For many political scientists, the first step in analyzing and reporting information involves the analysis and presentation of frequency tables that depict the distributions of the variables of concern. A frequency distribution is nothing more than a tabulation of raw data according to numerical values and discrete classes. A frequency distribution of religious association, for example, shows the number of individuals belonging to a particular religious group. As an example, produce a frequency distribution for the political party affiliation of U.S. presidents. Before you start, make sure you are familiar with Chapter 1, Getting Started.

→ Data File: **PRESIDENTS**
→ Task: **ANALYZE—DESCRIPTIVE STATISTICS—FREQUENCIES**
→ Variable: **PARTY**
→ View: **FREQUENCIES**

If you followed the SPSSW Guide correctly, you should have produced a frequency distribution like the one in Figure 2-1. The figure shows that 43 men have served as president of the United States. It also shows that more Republicans (18) have filled the position than any other political party. The percentage of the data representing each party is also reflected. As you can see, more than 32 percent of American presidents belonged to the Democratic Party (32.6 percent). Because the variable is a nominal level variable, the cumulative percentage is not that meaningful. You could say though that over 74 percent of the presidents belonged to one of the current major parties. When there are missing cases in the distribution, the Valid Percent column will differ from the Cumulative Percent column. Now, it's time to produce some other frequency tables.

2-2a Exercise One: Frequency Distribution Analysis

Article II of the United States Constitution states "*No person except a natural-born citizen shall be eligible to the office of President; neither shall any person be eligible to that office who shall not have attained to the age of thirty-five years, and been fourteen years a resident within the United States.*" These are the only Constitutional qualifications to become President of the United States and millions of Americans meet these requirements. But what are the qualifications to perform the duties of the presidency? Presidents serve as administrative head of the nation, convene Congress, veto legislation, appoint officials, make treaties, and grant pardons to individuals who have committed offenses against the United States. In addition, presidents act as commander-in-chief of the military. But how do these limited constitutional qualifications prepare someone to head the armed forces? Should presidents be required to have served in the military so that they have some experience that will help them perform this vital duty? Does the public expect presidents to be successful when serving in the military? These questions may be examined by analyzing the military service records of American presidents. To

3. Most respondents were interviewed in the ___ region.
a. East
b. Midwest
c. South
d. West

Figure 2-6 reflects the political viewpoint of respondents who participated in a national survey.

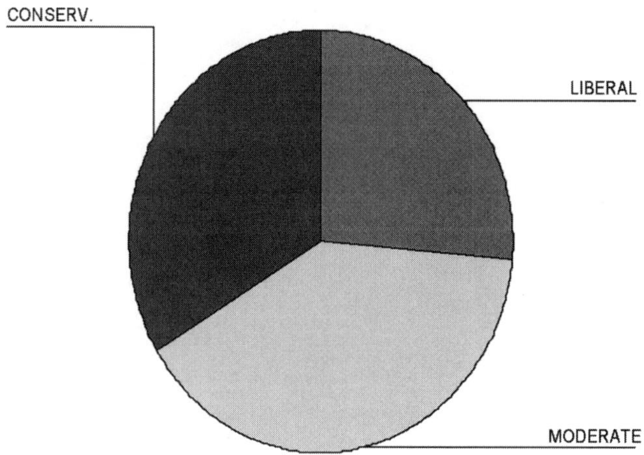

Figure 2-6
Political Viewpoint

4. Most respondents stated they were
a. conservative.
b. liberal.
c. moderate.
d. Most respondents did not indicate their political view.

5. A measure of ___ is a number that represents the principal value of a distribution of data.
a. dispersion
b. association
c. central tendency
d. variance

6. Political scientists use measures of ___ to reflect the amount of deviation of individual scores from the average value to indicate how well the measure of ___ summarizes the data.
a. dispersion; variation
b. central tendency; dispersion
c. dispersion; central tendency
d. central tendency; association

7. You can use the ___ to select the appropriate statistics you need when analyzing a single variable.
a. *Frequencies* dialog box
b. Variable View option
c. *View* menu
d. *Utilities* menu

8. What is the appropriate measure of central tendency to use with the following frequency distribution?

Gender of Respondent	Number	Percentage
Male	800	40
Female	1200	60

a. the mode
b. the median
c. the mean
d. the standard deviation

9. What is the appropriate measure of central tendency to use with the following frequency distribution?

Quality of Life	Number	Percentage
Poor	100	10
Good	600	60
Excellent	300	30

a. the mode
b. the median
c. the mean
d. the standard deviation

10. The mean for a particular test was 70. The high and low scores were 100 and 25. Thus, there is ___ dispersion between the mean and the extreme scores.
a. no
b. very little
c. moderate
d. a great deal of

Chapter

Chapter 3

Bivariate Statistics

Outline

3-1 Introduction

In the previous workbook chapter, tools and useful measures for summarizing and describing a single variable were discussed. The purpose of this workbook chapter is to help you understand the basics of bivariate statistics. Before you start working on the exercises in this chapter, you should have a thorough understanding of Chapters 10 and 14 in your textbook.

Political scientists are interested in analyzing relationships among variables. They may want to determine those factors associated with legislative voting behavior, change in the number of minorities and women living in a state, as well as support for a particular government program. In other words, they want to know the degree to which knowledge of one variable helps them to understand another variable.

In this chapter, you will examine some useful ways to analyze the relationships among two variables. This is called bivariate analysis because only two variables at a time are analyzed.

3-2 Statistical Significance and Hypothesis Testing

In Chapter 14 of the textbook, hypotheses and the need to determine whether observed relationships were statistically significant was discussed. In other words, how likely is it that a relationship found in sample data actually depicts a relationship in the population from which the sample was drawn? This question is important because it is the population, not the sample, that is being scrutinized. Samples are only drawn because it is often impractical or impossible to gather data about the entire population. Thus, the sample is only important to the extent that it allows meaningful predictions about the entire population to be made. Statisticians want to know whether the relationship is statistically significant, whether the relationship is substantial, and whether the relationship is causal.

Political scientists use a test of statistical significance in conjunction with hypothesis testing to infer properties of the population based on the analysis of sample data. These tools help them decide whether they can generalize an observed relationship between variables in a probability sample to the population from which they selected the sample.

As a reminder, statistical significance tests should only be used when analyzing the data from a probability sample. It is inappropriate to use these tests to examine relationships from other types of samples or when working with the entire population in lieu of a sample of the population. If data is available about all the cases in a population, for example, census data for the 50 states, the population is already known. There is no need to generalize based on an analysis of data. Having said this, many political scientists sometimes consider statistical significance tests to help them examine the importance of their results. This is especially so when the total number of cases in the population is rather small, for example the American states, the presidents, and members of the U.S. Senate.

3-3 Contingency Tables and Measures of Association for Nonmetric Data

A contingency table, also known as a cross-tabulation table, depicts the relationship between two variables by displaying all the combinations of categories of the variables. Political scientists often use contingency tables to analyze the relationship between variables that are measured at the nominal or ordinal level. You determine the size of a contingency table by determining the number of values for the row (dependent) variable and the number of values for the column (inde-

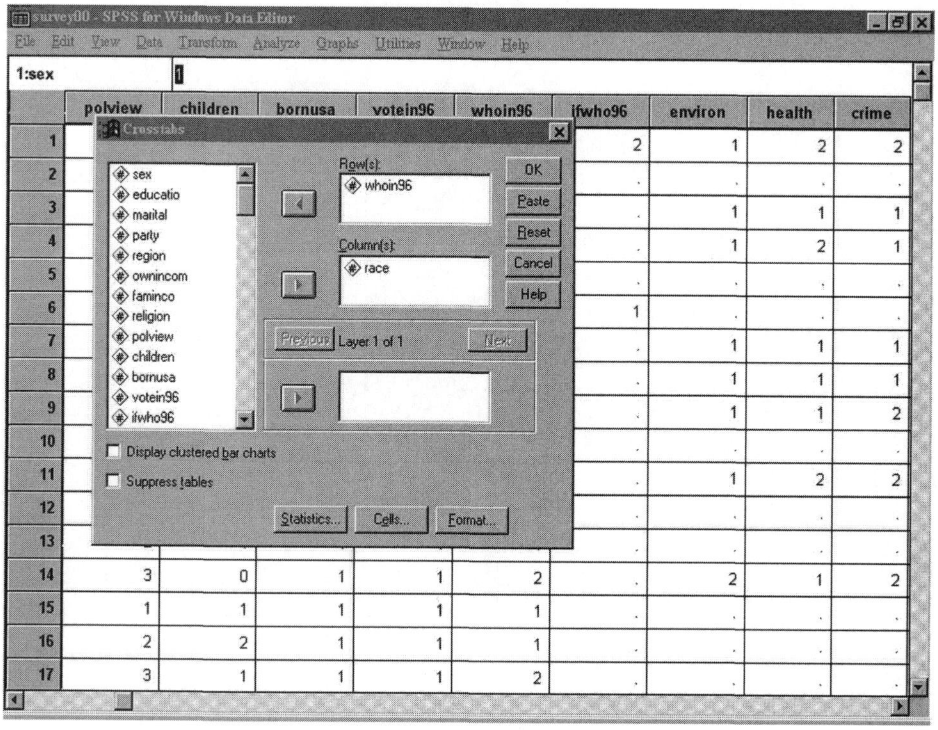

Figure 3-1
Crosstabs Dialog Box

pendent) variable. If there are two values of the row variable and three values of the column variable, for example, the table is a 2 by 3 table.

Look at a contingency table that depicts the relationship between voting choice and race.

→ Data File: **SURVEY**
→ Task: **ANALYZE—DESCRIPTIVE STATISTICS—CROSSTABS**
→ Row Variable: **WHOIN96**
→ Column Variable: **RACE**

If you followed the SPSSW Guide correctly, you will see the *Crosstabs* dialog box depicted in Figure 3-1 on your computer screen.

To continue the analysis you need to determine the appropriate statistic to use. Then, you need to click on the *Statistics* button to select the appropriate statistic. Recall from Chapter 14 of your textbook that there are several measures of association you can use to determine relationships in your data. Each measure also has its own application. That is, the level of measurement, size of the table (2 by 2, 2 by 3, etc.), and the direction of the relationship dictate which measure you should use. In this example, each variable is measured at the nominal level, there are three rows and two columns (3 by 2 table), and the relationship is nondirectional (symmetrical). Based on this information and Table 14-11 of your textbook, the Cramer's V statistic is the appropriate measure to use with the table. As such, choose the ***Phi and CRAMER's V*** statistics in the *Crosstabs: Statistics* dialog box. Clicking on the button will produce Figure 3-2.

To complete your analysis, you should also click on the Cells button and select the column percentages option. This will allow you to compare and examine differences between the percentages depicted across categories of the independent variable. Thus, the last part of the SPSSW Guide for this exercise example is:

→ View 1: **STATISTICS—PHI and CRAMER'S V**
→ View 2: **CELLS—PERCENTAGE—COLUMN**

Figure 3-2
Crosstabs: Statistics
Dialog Box

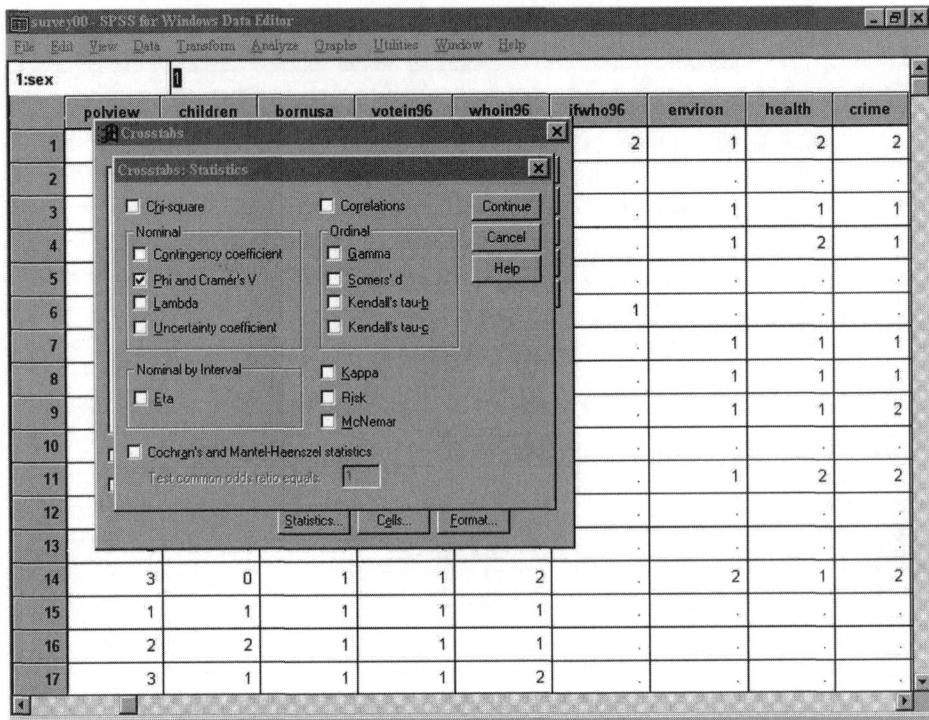

After you complete the previous step, the program will produce the output depicted in Figure 3-3.

The Case Processing Summary table shows the *total* number of cases included in the data set (N = 2817). The table also shows that a little over 56 percent of the cases were analyzed (***Valid*** N =1590). The other 1227 [***Missing***] cases were not included because the respondents did not respond to the voting question, were not asked to respond to the question, or voted for some other candidate in the 1996 Presidential election.

The column marginal frequencies in the 3 by 2 contingency table display the number of whites (1352) and blacks (238) that voted for one of the candidates. The table also shows that 888 (55.8 percent) people voted for Clinton, 488 (30.7 percent) for Dole, and 214 (13.5 percent) for Perot. These totals represent the row marginal frequencies. The table's cells also reflect the number and percentage of votes received from each racial group for each candidate. For example, 224 or 94.1 percent of the black voters cast their vote for Clinton. On the other hand 664 or 49.1 percent of the white voters cast their vote for Clinton.

The Cramer's V statistic is the appropriate statistic to use with this table. The Symmetric Measures table shows that the value is .323. To interpret the value you need to refer to Table 14-8 in your textbook. For this example, there is a moderate relationship between a vote in the 1996 Presidential election and the voter's race.

The Symmetric Measures table also presents the approximate significance of the relationship. In this example the relationship is highly significant with a significance level of $p < .000$. Thus, it can be said that there is both a substantive and a statistical relationship between the two variables.

3-3a Exercise One: Cross-Tabulation Analysis

In this exercise, you will determine whether there is, in a sample survey of adult Americans, a relationship between an individual's level of education and the amount of time that individual spends reading the newspaper. Before you try to

Figure 3-3
Cross-Tabulation Output

Case Processing Summary

	Cases					
	Valid		Missing		Total	
	N	Percent	N	Percent	N	Percent
Did you vote for Clinton, Dole or Perot? * Respondent's race.	1590	56.4%	1227	43.6%	2817	100.0%

Did you vote for Clinton, Dole or Perot? * Respondent's race. Cross-tabulation

			Respondent's race.		Total
			WHITE	BLACK	
Did you vote for Clinton, Dole or Perot?	CLINTON	Count	664	224	888
		% within Respondent's race.	49.1%	94.1%	55.8%
	DOLE	Count	479	9	488
		% within Respondent's race.	35.4%	3.8%	30.7%
	PEROT	Count	209	5	214
		% within Respondent's race.	15.5%	2.1%	13.5%
Total		Count	1352	238	1590
		% within Respondent's race.	100.0%	100.0%	100.0%

Symmetric Measures

		Value	Approx. Sig.
Nominal by Nominal	Phi	.323	.000
	Cramer's V	.323	.000
N of Valid Cases		1590	

a Not assuming the null hypothesis.
b Using the asymptotic standard error assuming the null hypothesis.

determine whether there is a relationship, state a research and a null hypothesis for the relationship that you expect to find between the two variables.

Research Hypothesis:

Null Hypothesis:

→ Data File: **SURVEY**
→ Task: **ANALYZE—DESCRIPTIVE STATISTICS—CROSSTABS**
→ Row Variable: **NEWSPAPE**
→ Column Variable: **EDUCATIO**
→ View 1: **STATISTICS—KENDALL'S TAU B**
→ View 2: **CELLS—PERCENTAGE—COLUMN**

After you examine the SPSSW output, respond to the following questions.

1. What is the level of data for the dependent variable (**NEWSPAPE**)?

Nominal **Ordinal** **Interval** **Ratio**

2. What is the level of data for the independent variable (**EDUCATIO**)?

Nominal **Ordinal** **Interval** **Ratio**

3. How many rows are in the table?

4. How many columns are in the table?

5. Is the relationship a directional one?

Y N

6. What is the value of the Kendall's tau-b statistic for this relationship?

7. According to the statistic, by what percentage has the number of errors been reduced in predicting newspaper reading by knowing the individual's level of education?

8. Is this relationship statistically significant?

Y N

9. Do you reject the null hypothesis?

Y N

10. Based on these results, what would you conclude about the extent to which level of education is related to reading the newspaper?

3-4 Scatter Plots and Measures of Association for Metric Data

Political scientists often analyze a scatter plot when initially analyzing relationships between metric data. A scatter plot depicts the relationship between two variables by plotting on intersecting axes the points representing the dependent variable (y) and independent variable (x) observations for each case in the database.

Use SPSSW to produce a scatter plot that examines the effect that newspaper circulation has on the literacy rate of a nation's populace.

→ Data File: **NATIONS**
→ Task: **GRAPHS—SCATTER—SIMPLE**
→ Y Axis Variable: **LITERACY**
→ X Axis Variable: **PAPERS**
→ View: **GRAPH**

After you complete the above SPSSW Guide, the program will produce the output depicted in Figure 3-4.

Perusal of the scatter plot reveals that there appears to be a positive relationship between the two variables. In other words, the greater the level of newspaper circulation, the higher the nation's literacy rate (measured as number of literate individuals per 1000 residents over 15 years of age). However, you cannot tell how strong the relationship is or how accurately you can predict a nation's literacy rate by knowing the newspaper circulation rate. In addition, it cannot be determined whether the relationship is statistically significant. Thus, analysis of the two variables needs to continue so that these questions can be answered.

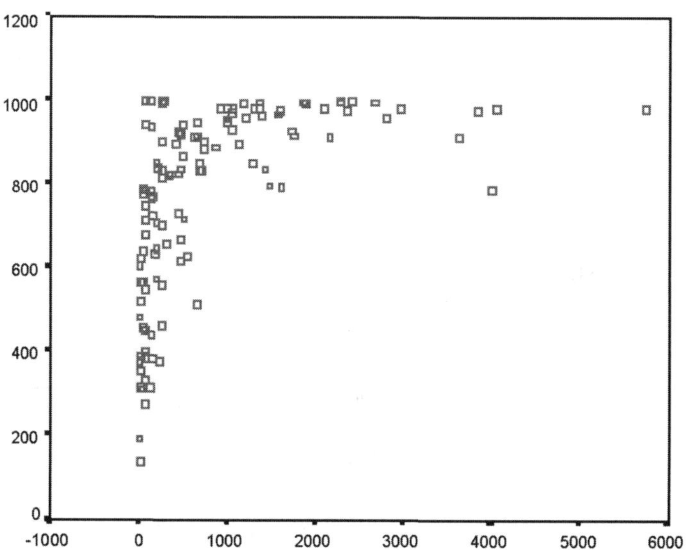

Figure 3-4
Scatter Plot

→ Data File: **NATIONS**
→ Task: **ANALYZE—REGRESSION—LINEAR**
→ Dependent Variable: **LITERACY**
→ Independent Variable: **PAPERS**
→ View: **REGRESSION**

Figure 3-5 shows the *Linear Regression* dialog box produced by the above SPSSW Guide.

You can produce the output shown in Figure 3-6 by clicking on the OK button in the upper right corner of the *Linear Regression* dialog box. The Variables Entered/Removed table depicts the variables included in the final regression model. Next, the Model Summary table presents some valuable information. The

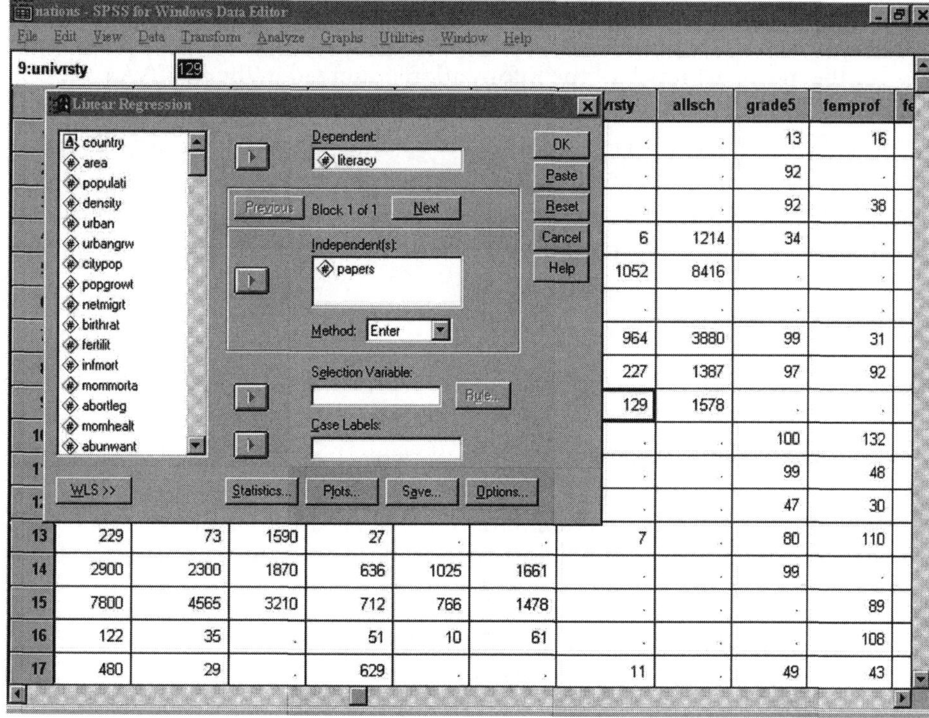

Figure 3-5
Linear Regression
Dialog Box

Figure 3-6
Regression Output

Variables Entered/Removed(b)

Model	Variables Entered	Variables Removed	Method
1	1994: Newspapers per 10,000 population.(a)	.	Enter

a All requested variables entered.
b Dependent Variable: 1995: Literacy rate. Number of people over 15 years of age able to both read and write per 1000 population.

Model Summary

Model	R	R Square	Adjusted R Square	Std. Error of the Estimate	Change Statistics				
					R Square Change	F Change	df1	df2	Sig. F Change
1	.514(a)	.265	.258	193.752	.265	42.118	1	117	.000

a Predictors: (Constant), 1994: Newspapers per 10,000 population.

ANOVA(b)

Model		Sum of Squares	df	Mean Square	F	Sig.
1	Regression	1581119.693	1	1581119.693	42.118	.000(a)
	Residual	4392159.097	117	37539.821		
	Total	5973278.79(	118			

a Predictors: (Constant), 1994: Newspapers per 10,000 population.
b Dependent Variable: 1995: Literacy rate. Number of people over 15 years of age able to both read and write per 1000 population.

Coefficients(a)

Model		Unstandardized Coefficients		Standardized Coefficients	t	Sig.
		B	Std. Error	Beta		
1	(Constant)	674.951	22.448		30.067	.000
	1994: Newspapers per 10,000 population.	.112	.017	.514	6.490	.000

a Dependent Variable: 1995: Literacy rate. Number of people over 15 years of age able to both read and write per 1000 population.

R, for example, is the value of the correlation coefficient (r = .514). The correlation coefficient gives an idea of the strength and direction of the relationship between the two variables. Again, when you refer to Table 14-8 in your textbook, you will find that there is a substantial positive relationship present. In addition, the R Square value (.265) suggests that newspaper circulation accounts for almost 27 percent of the variation in a nation's literacy rate.

For the most part much of the information presented in the ANOVA table can be ignored. The table does show, however, that the model is statistically significant. The Coefficients table provides much valuable information. Note that the table presents unstandardized regression coefficients and standardized coefficients. The unstandardized coefficients can be used to develop a regression equation to predict the level of literacy in a nation with a given newspaper circulation. Recall that the general bivariate regression equation is:

$$\hat{Y} = a + bx$$

where $\hat{Y}$ is the predicted literacy rate, and a represents the y-intercept. It is also called the *constant* and is represented as such in SPSSW computer printout results. The b is the unstandardized regression coefficient (also called the *slope*), and x is the actual newspaper circulation rate. You can use the information in Figure 3-6 to predict the literacy rate of a nation having a newspaper circulation rate of 110 newspapers per 1000 people by substituting the table's values into the general formula.

literacy rate = 675 + .112(110) = 675 + 12.3 = 687.3
(per 1000 residents 15 years of age or older).

Thus, in a nation having a circulation rate of 110 newspapers per 1000 people, you can predict that almost 69 percent of the people 15 years or older can read and write.

3-4a Exercise Two: Regression Analysis

Is there a relationship between the population density of a state and the number of AIDS- and HIV-related deaths in a state? Before you try to determine whether there is a relationship, state a research and a null hypothesis for the relationship that you expect to find between the two variables.

Research Hypothesis:

Null Hypothesis:

→ Data File:	**STATES**
→ Task:	**ANALYZE—REGRESSION—LINEAR**
→ Dependent Variable:	**AIDS**
→ Independent Variable:	**DENSITY**
→ View:	**REGRESSION**

Note: This exercise will not use a sample because the entire population of states is available (50 states). Therefore, questions dealing with statistical significance will be skipped to concentrate on the strength of the relationship.

After you examine the SPSSW output, respond to the following questions.

11. What is the value of the Pearson correlation coefficient (r)?

12. What is the value of the R-Square statistic?

13. According to the statistic, how much of the variation in a state's AIDS- and HIV-related deaths per 1000 people is accounted for by the population density?

14. What is the value of the Y intercept?

15. What is the value of the unstandardized regression coefficient (slope)?

16. Substitute the regression values/results into the regression equation. (For example, $Y = 20 + 5x$).

17. What is the predicted number of AIDS- and HIV-related deaths per 1000 people for a state having a population density of 100?

18. Based on these results, what would you conclude about the extent to which population density is related to AIDS- and HIV-related deaths?

Chapter Quiz

1. Political scientists use a test of ___ in conjunction with hypothesis testing to infer properties of the population based on the analysis of sample data.
   a. dispersion
   b. association
   c. statistical significance
   d. central tendency
2. A ___ depicts the relationship between two variables by displaying all the combinations of categories of the variables.
   a. frequencies table
   b. contingency table
   c. regression equation
   d. scatter plot

Use Table 3-1 to respond to Questions 3 and 4. The table shows the percentage of presidents who served in the military by their political party.

Table 3-1 Presidents Who Served in Military by Political Party

	Political Party		
Military Service?	**Other**	**Democratic**	**Republican**
Yes	45.5	50	66.7
No	55.5	50	33.3
Totals	11	14	18

3. What is the appropriate measure of association to use with the table?
   a. Phi
   b. Cramer's V
   c. Gamma
   d. Tau b
4. The table suggests that there is ___ relationship between the variables.
   a. no
   b. a weak
   c. a moderate
   d. a strong

Use Figure 3-7 to respond to Questions 5, 6, and 7. The scatter plot reflects the relationship between the average life expectancy in the nations of the world and the extent of AIDS-related cases (per 100,000 residents) throughout the world.

5. The plot suggests that there is a ___ relationship between the variables.
   a. positive but very weak
   b. negative but very weak
   c. negative and moderate
   d. negative and substantial
   e. There is no relationship.

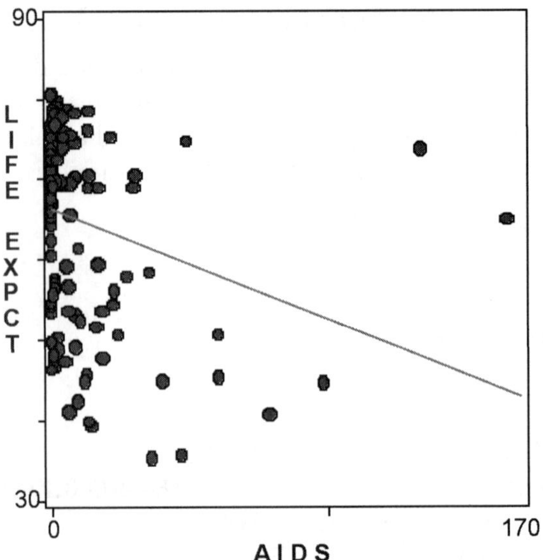

Figure 3-7
Average Life Expectancy by Extent of AIDS-Related Cases

6. Based on the scatter plot, what is the predicted life expectancy for a nation that has 100 AIDS cases per 100,000 residents?
   a. a little more than 66 years
   b. a little more than 52 years
   c. a little more than 80 years
   d. a little more than 26 years
7. The R-Square value for the above relationship between life expectancy and AIDS is .071. This value can be interpreted to suggest
   a. that there is no relationship between the variables.
   b. that the extent of AIDS in a nation accounts for a little more than seven percent of the variation in the life expectancy of a nation.
   c. that a nation's life expectancy will decrease with an increase in the number of AIDS cases in the nation.
   d. The statistic implies both b and c.

Use the following regression equation to respond to Questions 8 and 9. The regression equation depicts the relationship between the level of hate crimes in American cities (HC), the percentage of minorities living in American cities (M%), the school dropout rate in American cities (DROP%) and the population density of American cities (D).

$HC = 32 - .50\ (M\%) + .7\ (DROP\%) + 3\ (D)$

8. Which variable is the dependent variable?
   a. the level of hate crimes in American cities (HC)
   b. the percentage of minorities living in American cities (M%)
   c. the school dropout rate in American cities (DROP%)
   d. the population density of American Cities (D)
9. The beta values for each variable are: M% = –.35; DROP% = .25; D = .15. Based on the beta values, which variable is the most important for explaining the level of hate crimes in American cities?
   a. the school dropout rate in American cities
   b. the population density of American cities
   c. the percentage of minorities living in American cities
   d. There is no way to determine which variable is the most important one for explaining the level of hate crimes in American cities.
10. The probability for the relationship between property crime and the unemployment rate in American cities is $p < .03$. This result suggests
   a. there is a real relationship between the variables.
   b. there is a real but weak relationship between the variables.
   c. there is a real and substantial relationship between the variables.
   d. there is no real relationship between the variables.

Chapter 4

Multivariate Statistics

Outline

4-1 Introduction

To this point, the data analysis exercises have concentrated on the characteristics of a single variable (univariate analysis) and the isolated impact of one independent variable on a dependent variable (bivariate analysis). Political scientists, however, are also interested in assessing the relative and combined impacts of a number of independent variables on a dependent variable. The purpose of this workbook chapter is to help you understand the basics of multivariate analyses. Thus, the relative and combined impacts of variables related to the American public's support of the death penalty, factors contributing to health insurance coverage throughout America, and influences on the level of carbon-dioxide emissions throughout the world will be examined. Before you start working on the exercises in this chapter, you should have a thorough understanding of Chapter 15 in your textbook.

4-2 Multivariate Cross-Tabulation

As with bivariate analysis, cross-tabulation is used to analyze the impact of a control variable on the observed relationship between two variables measured at the nominal or ordinal level. After the relationship between two variables is determined, the control procedure requires that the original relationship between the independent and dependent variables for each category of the control variable be reexamined. This is done by reviewing the separate cross-tabulations (partial tables) that are produced for each category of a control variable.

4-2a Exercise One: Using Multivariate Cross-Tabulation to Explain Support for Capital Punishment

Is there a relationship between political party affiliation and support for capital punishment for convicted murderers in America? Before you try to determine whether there is a relationship, state a research and a null hypothesis for the relationship that you expect to find between the two variables.

Research Hypothesis:

Null Hypothesis:

→ Data File: **SURVEY**
→ Task: **ANALYZE—DESCRIPTIVE STATISTICS—CROSSTABS**
→ Row Variable: **EXECUTE**
→ Column Variable: **PARTY**
→ View 1: **STATISTICS—PHI and CRAMER'S V**
→ View 2: **CELLS—PERCENTAGE—COLUMN**

After you examine the SPSSW output, write the column percentages in Table 4-1.

1. Compare the percentages horizontally and describe the pattern.

2. What is the value of the Cramer's V statistic for this relationship?

Table 4-1 Support for Capital Punishment by Political Party

	Political Party Identification		
Support for Capital Punishment	**Democrats**	**Independents**	**Republicans**
Favor			
Oppose			

3. Is this relationship statistically significant?

Y **N**

4. Do you reject the null hypothesis?

Y **N**

5. Based on these results, what would you conclude about the extent to which political party affiliation is related to support of capital punishment in America?

You have seen that in America there is a relationship between political party affiliation and support for capital punishment. The relationship, however, is not a perfect one. There are Republicans opposed to and supportive of the death penalty and Democrats who support and oppose capital punishment. What other variables might affect this relationship? One possibility is race. The relationship between party affiliation and support for capital punishment might vary between different racial groups. African Americans, for example, may be more opposed to the death penalty regardless of their political party affiliation. Analyze the data to see if this is true.

→ Data File: **SURVEY**
→ Task: **ANALYZE—DESCRIPTIVE STATISTICS—CROSSTABS**
→ Row Variable: **EXECUTE**
→ Column Variable: **PARTY**
→ Control Variable: **RACE**
→ View 1: **STATISTICS—PHI and CRAMER'S V**
→ View 2: **CELLS—PERCENTAGE—COLUMN**

Notice that the above SPSSW Guide includes an additional component: → Control Variable: **RACE.** To complete this task, refer to Figure 4-1 which shows the *Crosstabs* dialog box. Note there is a button and list box beneath the words "Layer 1 of 1." To select the race variable for analysis, you need to highlight the variable in the variable list box at the left and click on the arrow button next to the Layer 1 of 1 list box.

After you examine the SPSSW output, write the column percentages in Tables 4-2 and 4-3 and respond to the questions that follow.

Figure 4-1
Crosstabs Dialog Box with Control Variable Selected

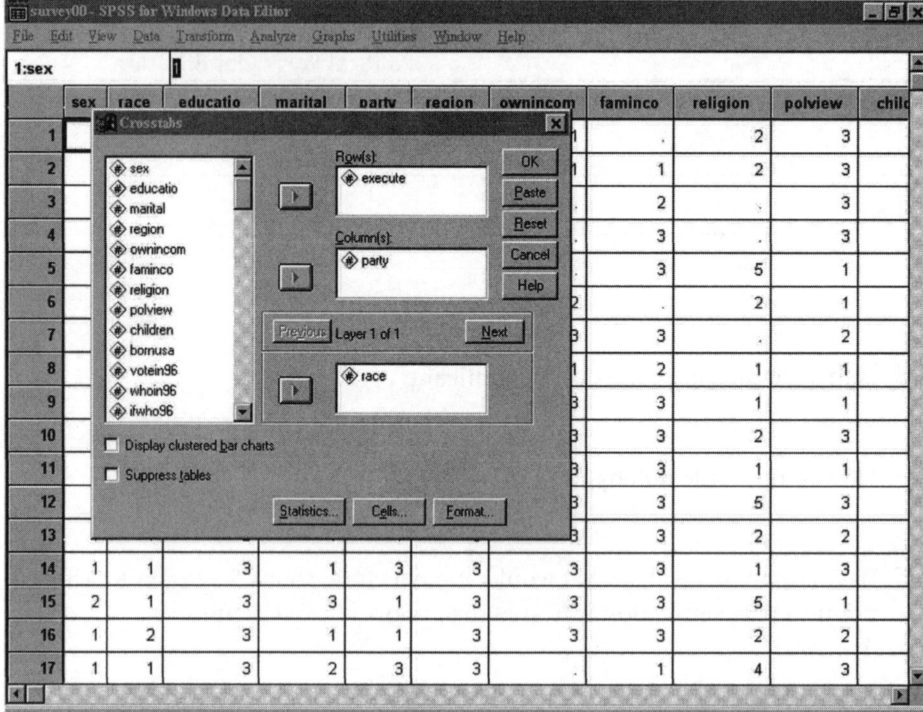

Table 4-2 Support for Capital Punishment by Political Party: White Respondents (%)

	Political Party Identification		
Support for Capital Punishment	**Democrats**	**Independents**	**Republicans**
Favor			
Oppose			

6. Compare the percentages horizontally and describe the pattern.

7. What is the value of the Cramer's V statistic for this relationship?

8. Is this relationship statistically significant?

Y **N**

Table 4-3 Support for Capital Punishment by Political Party: Black Respondents (%)

	Political Party Identification		
Support for Capital Punishment	**Democrats**	**Independents**	**Republicans**
Favor			
Oppose			

9. Compare the percentages horizontally and describe the pattern.

10. What is the value of the Cramer's V statistic for this relationship?

11. Is this relationship statistically significant?

Y N

12. Based on the results depicted in Tables 4-2 and 4-3, what would you conclude about the extent to which political party affiliation is related to support of capital punishment in America when controlling for race?

4-3 Partial Correlation

Political scientists use the partial-correlation procedure with metric-level data. This procedure is not as cumbersome to use as cross tabulations. For example, unlike cross tabulations, a single statistic is used to determine relationships. In addition, more than one variable can be controlled simultaneously. The procedure extends the logic of simple regression in that knowledge of an independent variable helps to predict values of a linear dependent variable.

4-3a Exercise Two: Using Partial Correlation to Identify Factors Contributing to Health Insurance Coverage throughout America

Lyndon Johnson used his public support following the death of President Kennedy to persuade Congress to become active in the War on Poverty. In addition, President Johnson created another role for the federal government in financing health care for Americans. Consequently Congress passed the Medicare Act of 1965 which created Medicare, a social insurance program, and Medicaid, a public assistance program. While each program pertains to certain groups of Americans, neither program is as extensive as those in many other industrial nations. Part of the reason for this is perhaps concern about an intrusive government along with a reliance on the private sector to provide most goods and services. In fact, the private health insurance industry in the United States is big business and many people would like to see government decrease its role in financing health care for Americans.

But what would the effect be if these medical assistance programs were reduced or discontinued? Would some Americans go without health coverage? To help answer these questions, examine the extent of private health insurance coverage throughout the United States.

→ Data File: **STATES**
→ Task: **ANALYZE—DESCRIPTIVE STATISTICS—FREQUENCIES**
→ Variable: **NOHLTHIN**
→ View: **STATISTICS—MEAN—MEDIAN—STD. DEVIATION**

After you examine the SPSSW output, answer the following questions.

13. What is the value of the mean?

14. What is the value of the median?

15. What is the value of the standard deviation?

16. Which measure of central tendency is the appropriate one to use? Or does it matter?

17. Based on these results, what would you conclude about the extent of health insurance coverage in America?

The results of the above SPSSW Guide suggest that there is some variation in the extent of health insurance coverage in the United States. What factors help to explain this variation? Health care is expensive, so perhaps the extent of poverty is a contributing factor. Before you try to determine whether there is a relationship, state a research and a null hypothesis for the relationship that you expect to find between the two variables.

Note: A sample will not be used in this exercise, since the entire population of states is available. Therefore, questions dealing with statistical significance can be skipped in order to concentrate on the strength of the relationship.

Research Hypothesis:

Null Hypothesis:

→ Data File: **STATES**
→ Task: **ANALYZE—CORRELATE—BIVARIATE**
→ Variable 1: **NOHLTHIN**
→ Variable 2: **POOR**
→ View: **CORRELATION COEFFICIENTS—PEARSON**

After you examine the SPSSW output, answer the following questions.

18. What is the value of the Pearson correlation coefficient?

19. Based on these results, what would you conclude about the extent to which poverty is related to health insurance coverage in America?

Poverty does influence the extent of health insurance coverage. But is the observed relationship a causal one? Or is it merely coincidental? Maybe some people do not have private health insurance because they rely on public health care. Thus, the extent of public health care coverage could affect the original relationship.

→ Data File: **STATES**
→ Task: **ANALYZE—DESCRIPTIVE STATISTICS—CORRELATE—PARTIAL**
→ Variable 1: **NOHLTHIN**
→ Variable 2: **POOR**
→ Controlling for: **HLTH$**
→ View: **CORRELATION COEFFICIENTS—PEARSON**

After you examine the SPSSW output, answer the following questions.

20. How many states are included in the analysis?

21. What is the value of the Pearson correlation coefficient?

22. Based on these results, what would you conclude about the extent to which poverty is related to health insurance coverage in America when controlling for public health assistance?

4-4 Multiple Regression

In Chapter 15 of the textbook you learned that the general regression equation for multivariate analysis is an extension of the simple regression equation. The procedure is used with metric-level data. Political scientists use multiple regression in an effort to explain as much variation in a dependent variable as possible.

4-4a Exercise Three: Using Multiple Regression to Explain Carbon-Dioxide Emissions around the World

People throughout the world are concerned about the effects of carbon-dioxide emissions. In addition, many of the world's top scientists have determined that global warming is a direct result of carbon dioxide and other greenhouse gases released when fossil fuels are burned. Examine the effect that automobile-based transportation has on the extent of carbon-dioxide emissions throughout the world. Before you try to determine whether there is a relationship, state a research and a null hypothesis for the relationship that you expect to find between the two variables.

Research Hypothesis:

Null Hypothesis:

→ Data File: **NATIONS**
→ Task: **ANALYZE—REGRESSION—LINEAR**
→ Dependent Variable: **GREENHOU**
→ Independent Variable: **HWYVEH**
→ View: **REGRESSION**

After you examine the SPSSW output, respond to the following questions.

23. What is the value of the Pearson correlation coefficient (R)?

24. What is the value of the R-Square statistic?

25. According to the statistic, how much of the variation in a nations' carbon dioxide emissions is accounted for by the number of vehicles on the roads?

26. What is the value of the Y intercept?

27. What is the value of the unstandardized regression coefficient (slope)?

28. Use the results to depict the regression equation.

You have seen that highway traffic in a nation contributes to the carbon-dioxide emission rate. What other factors might help to explain more variation in the emission rate? In addition to the number of vehicles on the roads, examine the effects of industrial production, electricity consumption, and urbanism.

→ Data File: **NATIONS**
→ Task: **ANALYZE—REGRESSION—LINEAR**
→ Dependent Variable: **GREENHOU**
→ Independent Variable 1: **HWYVEH**
→ Independent Variable 2: **INDGROWT**
→ Independent Variable 3: **ELECTRIC**
→ Independent Variable 4: **URBAN**
→ View: **REGRESSION**

After you examine the SPSSW output, respond to the following questions.

29. What percentage of the variation in a nation's emission rate is explained by the variables?

30. Write the unstandardized regression coefficient for each variable below.

HWYVEH ____________
INDGROWT ____________
ELECTRIC ____________
URBAN ____________

31. Write the beta coefficients for each variable below.

HWYVEH ____________
INDGROWT ____________
ELECTRIC ____________
URBAN ____________

32. In Chapter 15 of the textbook you read that the beta coefficient shows how many standard deviations of change are produced in the dependent variable by one standard deviation of change in an independent variable while controlling for the effects of the other independent variables. Considering this, which of the independent variables has the greatest effect on a nation's carbon-dioxide emission rate?
Which independent variable has the least effect?

Although the entire population is available, examine the results as if you were working a sample.

33. Is each of the variables statistically significant?

Y **N**

34. Which variable(s) is/are not statistically significant?

When you have a variable that is not statistically significant in a model, the proper procedure is to rerun the regression procedure without the variable that is not significant. Go ahead and do this.

35. Which independent variable has the greatest effect in the new regression model?

36. What percentage of the variation in a nation's emission rate is explained by the variables?

Chapter Quiz

1. After political scientists have determined the relationship between two variables, the ___ procedure requires them to reexamine the original relationship between the independent and dependent variables for each category of another variable.
a. correlation
b. statistical significance
c. control
d. scatter plot

2. Political scientists use the partial-correlation procedure with ___-level data.
a. nominal
b. ordinal
c. metric
d. all of the above

3. The following is the general form of the linear multiple regression model.
$\hat{Y} = a + B_1 X_1 + B_2 X_2 + B_3 X_3 + B_i X_i + e$
Which symbol represents the Y intercept?
a. $\hat{Y}$
b. a
c. B_1
d. e

4. The R-Squared (R^2) is known as the
a. correlation coefficient.
b. coefficient of determination.
c. coefficient of multiple determination.
d. Student's T-test.

5. ___ techniques are important because they help you to clarify the critical issue of causation and to directly address the notion of non-spuriousness.
a. Instrumentation
b. Control
c. Testing
d. Triangulation

6. When using the t-test to determine the statistical significance of the relationship between variables, the null hypothesis is symbolically written as
   a. Ho: X5 = 0.
   b. Ha: X5 = 0.
   c. Ho: T = 0.
   d. Ha: T = 0.
7. Based on the following beta coefficients for four independent variables, which variable is the most important for explaining variation in the dependent variable?

Variable	Beta Coefficient Value
1	.17
2	.27
3	−.40
4	.40

   a. Variable 1
   b. Variable 2
   c. Variable 3
   d. Variables 3 and 4
8. ___ are standardized coefficients in the regression equation that have been translated to a uniform scale and can easily be used to compare the relative influence of the variables.
   a. Coefficients of determination
   b. Degrees of freedom
   c. Pearson correlation coefficients
   d. Beta coefficients
9. ___ is a technique for measuring the mathematical relationships between more than one independent variable and a dependent variable, while controlling for the effect of all other independent variables in the equation.
   a. Simple correlation
   b. Multiple regression
   c. Cross-tabulation
   d. Scatter plot analysis
10. ___ are coefficients generated by the multiple regression routine. They represent the amount of change in the dependent variable associated with each independent variable, holding all other independent variables constant.
   a. Beta coefficients
   b. Chi-square statistics
   c. Partial slopes
   d. Lambda statistics

Chapter 5

An Overview of the Political World

Outline

5-1 Introduction

People constantly strive to improve their lives. Many aspire to insure that the social, economic, and political influences they experience do not negatively affect their lives. Since governments by definition influence people, this leads to the question: Which form of government is best? Answering this question is a difficult but important task for political scientists. As discussed in Chapter 4 of the textbook, philosophers, scholars, and political leaders have differed on how much government should control the people's behavior. Consequently, they have defined the *best government* differently throughout history. This exercise, however, will concentrate on a government by the many.

Table 4-3 in your textbook contrasts a polity and a democracy as forms of government by the many. The table shows that a polity is the good form of government by the many. A democracy, on the other hand, is the bad form of government by the many. The distinguishing factor is that one form rules in the interest of all (polity), while the other form rules in the interest of the rulers (democracy). Today, however, democracy exemplifies an optimal form of government that rules in the interest of the entire society. A direct form of democracy does not exist in today's world. Forms of a representative democracy may, however, be found. Thus, the purpose of this workbook chapter is to examine the extent, characteristics, and effect of representative democracy throughout the world. Before you start working on the exercises in this chapter, you should have a thorough understanding of Chapter 4 in the textbook.

5-2 Examining the Extent of Democracy

5-2a Exercise One

First, look at the extent of democracy throughout the world.

→ Data File: **NATIONS**
→ Task: **ANALYZE—DESCRIPTIVE STATISTICS—FREQUENCIES**
→ Variable: **DEMOCRAC**
→ View 1: **FREQUENCIES**
→ View 2: **STATISTICS—MEAN—MEDIAN—MODE**

Here the variable is an Index of Democracy assigned to several world nations. The higher the index score for a nation, the more political freedom (democratic) exists in the nation. After you are familiar with the frequencies distribution, answer the following questions.

1. What is the level of measurement for this variable?

2. What is the modal response for this variable?

3. What is the value of the median for this variable?

4. What is the value of the mean for this variable?

5. What is the best measure of central tendency to use for this variable?

6. What is the percentage of nations having a score of 4 or less on the scale?

7. What do the results suggest about the extent of democracy throughout the world?

5-3 Examining Possible Characteristics of Democracy

5-3a Exercise Two

Over the years, numerous political scientists have identified several fundamental principles of representative democracy. These principles include popular sovereignty, majority rule, political equality, and political liberty. While governments can abuse these principles, they are still principles to strive for. Many world nations do not incorporate these principles in their governments. Nor have they established substantive policies supporting such civil liberties as freedom of speech and freedom of association, which create the necessary conditions for the practice of democracy. For this exercise, we will examine several variables that characterize a democratic form of government.

→ Data File: **NATIONS**
→ Task: **ANALYZE—DESCRIPTIVE STATISTICS—FREQUENCIES**
→ Variable: **CIVILLIB**
→ View 1: **FREQUENCIES**
→ View 2: **STATISTICS—MEAN—MEDIAN—MODE**
→ View 3: **CHARTS—BAR CHARTS**

Here the variable is an Index of Civil Liberties assigned to several world nations. The higher the index score for a nation, the greater the extent of civil liberties in the nation. After you are familiar with the bar chart, answer the following questions.

8. What is the level of measurement for this variable?

9. How many nations had a score of 4 on the scale?

10. How many nations are represented by the Least Free bar?

11. How many nations are represented by the Most Free bar?

12. What do the results suggest about the extent of civil liberties throughout the world?

Look at a pie chart that depicts the level of freedom of association in these nations.

→ Data File: **NATIONS**
→ Task: **ANALYZE—DESCRIPTIVE STATISTICS—FREQUENCIES**
→ Variable: **FOAC**
→ View 1: **FREQUENCIES**
→ View 2: **STATISTICS—MEAN—MEDIAN—MODE**
→ View 3: **CHARTS—PIE CHARTS**

Here the variable is an Index of Freedom of Association. This variable was created by combining the extent of boycott and demonstration activity in the nations of the world. The lower the index score for a nation, the lower the extent of association in the nation. After you are familiar with the bar chart, answer the following questions.

13. What is the level of measurement for this variable?

14. How many nations were included in the analysis?

15. What is the appropriate measure of central tendency to use?

16. What do the results suggest about the extent of association throughout the world?

Continue your analysis of world democracy by examining a variable that measures the extent of signing a petition in several world nations.

→ Data File: **NATIONS**
→ Task: **ANALYZE—DESCRIPTIVE STATISTICS—FREQUENCIES**
→ Variable: **PETITION**
→ View 1: **FREQUENCIES**
→ View 2: **STATISTICS—MEAN—MEDIAN—MODE**
→ View 3: **CHARTS—HISTOGRAM**

Here the variable measures the extent of petitioning throughout the world. After you are familiar with the histogram, answer the following questions.

17. What is the level of measurement for this variable?

18. What is the modal response for this variable?

19. What is the value of the median for this variable?

20. What is the value of the mean for this variable?

21. What is the best measure of central tendency to use for this variable?

22. Looking at the histogram, how many nations report a petitioning rate between 5 and 15 percent?

23. What essential principle of a democracy (good form of government by the many) does the variable measure (be specific)?

24. What do the results suggest about the extent of petitioning throughout the world?

Now identify some variables that characterize a democratic government.

→ Data File: **NATIONS**
→ Task: **ANALYZE—DESCRIPTIVE STATISTICS—CROSSTABS**
→ Row Variable: **CDEMOCR**
→ Column Variable: **CIVLIBC**
→ View 1: **STATISTICS—KENDALL'S TAU B**
→ View 2: **CELLS—PERCENTAGE—COLUMN**

Here the independent variable measures the extent of civil liberties in a nation.

Note: A sample will not be used in this exercise; the entire population of nations is available (174 nations). Therefore, questions dealing with statistical significance will be skipped to concentrate on the strength of the relationship.

25. Before you try to determine whether there is a relationship, state a research and a null hypothesis for the relationship that you expect to find between the two variables.

Research Hypothesis:

Null Hypothesis:

After you examine the SPSSW output, write the column percentages in Table 5-1.

Table 5-1 Extent of Democracy by Extent of Civil Liberties (%)

	Extent of Civil Liberties			
Extent of Democracy	**Very Limited**	**Limited**	**Somewhat High**	**Very High**
Least Democratic				
Somewhat Democratic				
Democratic				
Most Democratic				

26. Compare the percentages horizontally and describe the pattern.

27. What is the value of the Kendall's tau-b statistic for this relationship?

28. Give a proportional reduction of error interpretation of these results.

29. Based on these results, what would you conclude about the extent to which democracy is characterized by expanded civil liberties in a nation?

→ Data File: **NATIONS**
→ Task: **ANALYZE—DESCRIPTIVE STATISTICS—CROSSTABS**
→ Row Variable: **CDEMOCR**
→ Column Variable: **FOAC**
→ View 1: **STATISTICS—KENDALL'S TAU C**
→ View 2: **CELLS—PERCENTAGE—COLUMN**

Here the independent variable measures the extent of freedom to associate in a nation.

30. Before you try to determine whether there is a relationship, state a research and a null hypothesis for the relationship that you expect to find between the two variables.

Research Hypothesis:

Null Hypothesis:

After you examine the SPSSW output, write the column percentages in Table 5-2.

Table 5-2 Extent of Democracy by Extent of Freedom of Association (%)

	Extent of Freedom of Association		
Extent of Democracy	**Low**	**Moderate**	**High**
Least Democratic			
Somewhat Democratic			
Democratic			
Most Democratic			

31. Compare the percentages horizontally and describe the pattern.

32. What is the value of the Kendall's tau-c statistic for this relationship?

33. Give a Proportional Reduction of Error interpretation of these results.

34. Based on these results, what would you conclude about the extent to which democracy is characterized by expanded rights to associate in a nation?

→ Data File: **NATIONS**
→ Task: **ANALYZE—DESCRIPTIVE STATISTICS—CROSSTABS**
→ Row Variable: **CDEMOCR**
→ Column Variable: **PETITC**
→ View 1: **STATISTICS—KENDALL'S TAU B**
→ View 2: **CELLS—PERCENTAGE—COLUMN**

Here the independent variable measures the extent of petitioning in a nation. After you examine the SPSSW output, write the column percentages in Table 5-3.

Table 5-3 Extent of Democracy by Petitioning (%)

	Petitioning			
Extent of Democracy	**Very Low**	**Low**	**High**	**Very High**
Least Democratic				
Somewhat Democratic				
Democratic				
Most Democratic				

35. Before you try to determine whether there is a relationship, state a research and a null hypothesis for the relationship that you expect to find between the two variables.

Research Hypothesis:

Null Hypothesis:

36. Compare the percentages horizontally and describe the pattern.

37. What is the value of the Kendall's tau-b statistic for this relationship?

38. Give a Proportional Reduction of Error interpretation of these results.

39. Based on these results, what would you conclude about the extent to which democracy is characterized by petitioning in a nation?

40. Which of the variables is most characteristic of the extent of democracy in a nation?

    CIVLIBC FOAC PETITC

41. Which of the variables is the least characteristic of the extent of democracy in a nation?

    CIVLIBC FOAC PETITC

5-4 Examining the Effect of Democracy

5-4a Exercise Three

It stands to reason that conflict should be relatively low in a nation ruled by those ruling in the public interest. Continue your analysis of world democracy by examining the effect democracy has on the level of cultural conflict (**CONFLICT**) in a nation. Cultural conflict includes political conflict, violence, and/or warfare.

→ Data File: **NATIONS**
→ Task: **ANALYZE—DESCRIPTIVE STATISTICS—CROSSTABS**
→ Row Variable: **CONFLICT**
→ Column Variable: **CDEMOCR**
→ View 1: **STATISTICS—KENDALL'S TAU B**
→ View 2: **CELLS—PERCENTAGE—COLUMN**

42. Before you try to determine whether there is a relationship, state a research and a null hypothesis for the relationship that you expect to find between the two variables.

Research Hypothesis:

Null Hypothesis:

After you examine the SPSSW output, write the column percentages in Tables 5-4 through 5-7 and respond to the questions that follow.

Table **5-4 Type of Cultural Conflict by Extent of Democracy (%)**

	Extent of Democracy			
Type of Cultural Conflict	Least Democratic	Somewhat Democratic	Democratic	Most Democratic
None				
Political				
Violence				
Warfare				

43. Compare the percentages horizontally and describe the pattern.

44. What is the value of the Kendall's tau-b statistic for this relationship?

45. Give a Proportional Reduction of Error interpretation of these results.

46. Based on these results, what would you conclude about the extent to which democracy is related to cultural conflict in a nation?

Now continue your analysis of the effect democracy has on political unrest in a nation. For this exercise, you will analyze the effect that a diverse population has on the original relationship.

→ Data File: **NATIONS**
→ Task: **ANALYZE—DESCRIPTIVE STATISTICS—CROSSTABS**
→ Row Variable: **CONFLICT**
→ Column Variable: **CDEMOCR**
→ Control Variable: **CMULTICU**
→ View 1: **STATISTICS—KENDALL'S TAU B**
→ View 2: **CELLS—PERCENTAGE—COLUMN**

After you examine the SPSSW output, write the column percentages in Tables 5-5, 5-6, and 5-7 and respond to the questions that follow them.

Table 5-5 Type of Cultural Conflict by Extent of Democracy (%), Low Diversity

	Extent of Democracy			
Type of Cultural Conflict	Least Democratic	Somewhat Democratic	Democratic	Most Democratic
None				
Political				
Violence				
Warfare				

47. Compare the percentages horizontally and describe the pattern.

48. What is the value of the Kendall's tau-b statistic for this relationship?

49. Give a Proportional Reduction of Error interpretation of these results.

Table 5-6 Type of Cultural Conflict by Extent of Democracy (%), Moderate Diversity

	Extent of Democracy			
Type of Cultural Conflict	Least Democratic	Somewhat Democratic	Democratic	Most Democratic
None				
Political				
Violence				
Warfare				

50. Compare the percentages horizontally and describe the pattern.

51. What is the value of the Kendall's tau-b statistic for this relationship?

52. Give a Proportional Reduction of Error interpretation of these results.

53. Is this relationship statistically significant?

Y N

54. Do you reject the null hypothesis?

Y N

Table 5-7 Type of Cultural Conflict by Extent of Democracy (%), High Diversity

	Extent of Democracy			
Type of Cultural Conflict	Least Democratic	Somewhat Democratic	Democratic	Most Democratic
None				
Political				
Violence				
Warfare				

55. Compare the percentages horizontally and describe the pattern.

56. What is the value of the Kendall's tau-b statistic for this relationship?

57. Give a Proportional Reduction of Error interpretation of these results.

58. Based on the results depicted in Tables 5-5, 5-6, and 5-7, what would you conclude about the extent to which democracy is related to cultural conflict in a nation when controlling for population diversity?

Chapter Quiz

Use Table 5-8 to respond to Questions 1, 2, and 3. The table depicts the extent of personal political freedom throughout nations of the world.

Table 5-8 Extent of Individual Political Freedom

	Frequency	Percent	Valid Percent	Cumulative Percent
Valid				
Very low	30	17.2	17.5	17.5
Low	24	13.8	14.0	31.6
Somewhat low	13	7.5	7.6	39.2
Moderate	21	12.1	12.3	51.5
Somewhat high	21	12.1	12.3	63.7
High	25	14.4	14.6	78.4
Very high	37	21.3	21.6	100.0
Total	171	98.3	100.0	
Missing				
System	3	1.7		
Total	174	100.0		

1. What is the level of measurement for the variable?
   a. nominal
   b. ordinal
   c. interval
   d. ratio
2. What is the appropriate measure of central tendency to use with this variable?
   a. mode
   b. median
   c. mean
   d. Each measure of central tendency is appropriate to use.
3. What is the modal response for the variable?
   a. 13
   b. 24
   c. 27
   d. 37
   e. None of these choices is correct.

Use Figure 5-1 to respond to Questions 4, 5, and 6. The scatter plot depicts the relationship between the heterogeneity of a nation's population and voting turnout.

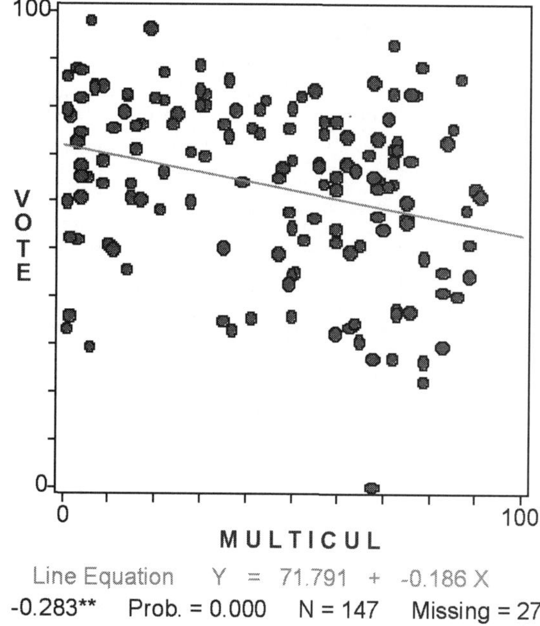

Line Equation Y = 71.791 + -0.186 X
-0.283** Prob. = 0.000 N = 147 Missing = 27

Figure 5-1
Population Heterogeneity by Voting Turnout

4. The scatter plot suggests that
   a. nations having a more diversified population will have higher voting turnouts.
   b. nations having a less diversified population will have higher voting turnouts.
   c. there is not a real relationship between the two variables.
   d. there is a real and substantial relationship between the two variables.
5. The regression equation suggests that voting turnout in a nation will
   a. increase by almost .2 percent with a more heterogeneous population.
   b. increase by almost 28 percent with a more heterogeneous population.
   c. decrease by almost .2 percent with a more heterogeneous population.
   d. decrease by almost 28 percent with a more heterogeneous population.
6. The scatter plot results suggest that the diversity of a nation's population will account for about ___ percent of a nation's voting turnout.
   a. 3
   b. 8
   c. 34
   d. 11

Use Table 5-9 to respond to Questions 7, 8, and 9. The table depicts the relationship between the extent of democracy in a nation and participation in a war.

Table 5-9 Participation in a War by Extent of Democracy

	Extent of Democracy			
	Least	**Somewhat**	**Democratic**	**Most**
None	40.7	44.1	65.2	81.1
Civil War	38.9	38.2	26.1	8.1
Interstate	20.4	17.6	8.7	10.8
Total #	54	34	46	37
Total %	100.0	100.0	100.0	100.0

7. The results suggest that there is ___ relationship between the variables.
   a. no
   b. a very weak
   c. a moderate
   d. a strong

8. What is the appropriate measure of association to use with the table?
   a. Phi
   b. Cramer's V
   c. Tau b
   d. Tau c

9. The probability for the table is p = < 0.000. Therefore you can assume that there
   a. is not a real relationship between the variables.
   b. is a real but weak relationship between the variables.
   c. is a real but moderate relationship between the variables.
   d. None of the above choices is correct.

10. Table 5-10 depicts the results of a multiple regression model used to explain voting turnout in a nation.

Table 5-10 Results of a Multiple Regression Model

Variable	Unstandardized b	Standardized Beta	t-statistic
Variable 1: Extent of national pride	0.118	0.145	0.851
Variable 2: Extent of civil liberties	–0.231	–0.282	–2.115**
Variable 3: Extent of multiculturalism	–0.430	–0.480	–2.542*
Variable 4: Region	–0.010	–0.015	–0.081

* p < . 05
** p < .01

Which variables are important for explaining voting turnout?
   a. Variable 1
   b. Variable 2
   c. Variable 3
   d. Variable 4
   e. Variables 2 and 3

Chapter 6

The American Political Process

Outline

6-1 Introduction

In many ways American politics is the most advanced subfield in the political science discipline. As stated in Chapter 5 of the textbook, there are several reasons for this. First, most scholars in the United States spend more time studying American politics than other subfields. Second, the democratic character of the United States allows scholars to have access to information that may not be available in other nations. You may have noticed, for example, that in the NATIONS data set, there were numerous *missing cases* for many of the variables. Third, there is an impressive financial commitment to research in many American universities. Consequently an impressive set of data collections relevant to virtually every aspect of politics and government in the United States is available. In this workbook chapter you will examine questions dealing with the value pursuits of government and components of the American political system such as linkage institutions and throughput institutions. Before you start working on the exercises in this chapter, you should have a thorough understanding of Chapter 5 in the textbook.

6-2 Examining the Value Pursuits of Government

6-2a Exercise One

Chapter 5 of your text emphasizes the importance of understanding America's cultural environment when analyzing the American political system. Such an understanding will help you to comprehend issues confronting the system and how the system operates. For example, Americans have different opinions about the values the government should pursue. Some believe that the major value pursuit of government is to maintain order. After all, throughout history, the maintenance of order was the first, and in many instances the last, reason for government. Individuals who stress this purpose support many of the government's actions in the aftermath of September 11, 2001.

Others are more concerned about individual freedom, or liberty. They oppose government actions that do not insure their position on this value. Consequently, they may oppose many of the government's actions in response to September 11. Thus, the American political environment challenges the political system to provide both freedom and order. The challenge is problematic because at some point the values of freedom and order conflict. Consider the following example that deals with freedom of speech.

The vast majority of Americans believe in the concept of free speech. Some even believe that this freedom is absolute. That is, Congress can make no law respecting freedom of speech. With the absolute interpretation, *no* means *no!* But what if an individual's speech could create hostility within a community? Should government limit that speech because of its duty to maintain order? Complete the following SPSSW Guide to examine the support Americans have toward certain speakers and their messages.

→ Data File: **SURVEY**
→ Task: **ANALYZE—DESCRIPTIVE STATISTICS—FREQUENCIES**
→ Variable 1: **ATHEISTS**
→ Variable 2: **RACISTSP**
→ Variable 3: **COMSPEAK**
→ Variable 4: **MILITSP**
→ Variable 5: **GAYSPEAK**
→ View 1: **FREQUENCIES**
→ View 2: **STATISTICS—MEAN—MEDIAN—MODE**

Note: The above SPSSW Guide will simultaneously produce a frequency table for each of the variables.

These variables measure the public's support for several controversial speakers: a person who is against religion (**ATHEISTS**); a person who believes blacks are genetically inferior (**RACISTSP**); a communist (**COMSPEAK**); a person who advocates ending elections and letting the military run the country (**MILITSP**); and someone who is gay (**GAYSPEAK**). After you are familiar with the frequency distributions, fill in Table 6-1 and answer the questions that follow.

Table 6-1 Support for Free Speech

Speaker	Number	Valid Percent
Atheist		
Racist		
Communist		
Military		
Gay		

1. What is the level of measurement for these variables?

2. Which of the speakers is more tolerated by the public?

3. Which of the speakers is the least tolerated by the public?

4. What is the value of the appropriate measure of central tendency for each variable?

5. Based on these results, what do you conclude about the level of support Americans have toward free speech?

As you can see from the table you completed, there is some divisiveness among Americans about promoting free speech. This raises an interesting question: What factors contribute to the difference in support? At the beginning of this workbook chapter, it was suggested that an understanding of the American cultural environment would help to answer many of the questions dealing with the American system of government. Based on this, it is possible that an individual's political ideology could influence that individual's attitude toward free speech. After all, many political scholars believe that someone's ideology can be predicted by the priority they place on the value pursuits of governments. Liberals, for example, may support free speech more than conservatives, who may be more concerned about the negative repercussions of controversial speeches. Examine the relationship between an individual's political ideology and that individual's support for free speech.

→ Data File: **SURVEY**
→ Task: **ANALYZE—DESCRIPTIVE STATISTICS—CROSSTABS**
→ Row Variable: **SPEAKCOL**
→ Column Variable: **POLVIEW**
→ View 1: **STATISTICS—PHI AND CRAMER'S V**
→ View 2: **CELLS—PERCENTAGE—COLUMN**

Note: The **SPEAKCOL** is an index variable that measures an individual's support for the speakers. Someone in the *very low* category, for example, is not tolerant of any of the speakers. On the other hand, someone in the *very high* category is tolerant of each speaker's right to speak in the community.

6. Before you try to determine whether there is a relationship, state a research and a null hypothesis for the relationship that you expect to find between the two variables.

Research Hypothesis:

Null Hypothesis:

After you examine the SPSSW output, write the column percentages in Table 6-2 and respond to the questions that follow.

Table 6-2 Support for Free Speech by Political Ideology %

Support for Free Speech	Liberal	Moderate	Conservative
Very Low			
Low			
High			
Very High			

7. Compare the percentages horizontally and describe the pattern.

8. What is the value of the Cramer's V statistic for this relationship?

9. Is this relationship statistically significant?

Y N

10. Do you reject the null hypothesis?

Y N

11. Based on these results, what do you conclude about the extent to which support for free speech is related to political ideology in America?

Throughout history, many Americans have been concerned about political equality in America. Many worried about *representation without taxation.* Minority groups struggled for the right to vote, the right to run for office, and the assurance that their vote counted the same in elections.

Later, various interests advocated the need to achieve socioeconomic equality. The development and support of public schools were seen as one way to foster equality of opportunity which would lead to socioeconomic equality. Others argued, however, that socioeconomic equality cannot be achieved without government support. For these individuals it is not enough to ensure equality of opportunity. Government must redistribute wealth and status to achieve socioeconomic equality. In other words, the political system must enact laws designed to produce *equality of result.* One way the American government has addressed this demand is to mandate affirmative action programs to recruit members of minority groups into professional schools and the workplace.

Equality of result is much more controversial than equality of opportunity. When the government redistributes wealth and status, it in effect creates winners and losers. The concept is also controversial because it conflicts with the demand for the government to insure freedom.

While many Americans see equality and freedom going hand in hand, the two values actually clash. Policies mandating special efforts to recruit, hire, and train minorities affect an employer's personnel choices. Thus, the American commitment to equality poses another difficult question for the political system: How much freedom should be sacrificed in trying to promote equality?

Examine the level of support Americans have for affirmative action programs.

→ Data File: **SURVEY**
→ Task: **ANALYZE—DESCRIPTIVE STATISTICS—FREQUENCIES**
→ Variable: **AFFRMACT**
→ View 1: **FREQUENCIES**
→ View 2: **STATISTICS—MEAN—MEDIAN—MODE**

After you are familiar with the resulting distribution, answer the following questions.

12. What is the level of measurement for this variable?

13. What is the appropriate measure of central tendency to use?

14. What is the value of the appropriate measure of central tendency?

15. What is the valid percentage of respondents who support affirmative action programs?

16. Based on these results, what do you conclude about Americans' support for affirmative action programs?

Although support for affirmative action in America is low, it does exist. Some Americans do support affirmative action initiatives. Who supports them? Since the programs are supposed to enhance the socioeconomic status of minority groups, see if members of a minority race support these programs more than white Americans.

→ Data File: **SURVEY**
→ Task: **ANALYZE—DESCRIPTIVE STATISTICS—CROSSTABS**
→ Row Variable: **AFFRMACT**
→ Column Variable: **RACE**
→ View 1: **STATISTICS—PHI AND CRAMER'S V**
→ View 2: **CELLS—PERCENTAGE—COLUMN**

17. Before you try to determine whether there is a relationship, state a research and a null hypothesis for the relationship that you expect to find between the two variables.

Research Hypothesis:

Null Hypothesis:

After you examine the SPSSW output, write the column percentages in Table 6-3 and respond to the questions that follow.

Table **6-3 Support for Affirmative Action by Race %**

Support for Affirmative Action	White	Black
Favor		
Oppose		

18. Compare the percentages horizontally and describe the pattern.

19. What is the value of the Cramer's V statistic for this relationship?

20. Is this relationship statistically significant?

Y N

21. Do you reject the null hypothesis?

Y N

22. Based on these results, what would you conclude about the extent to which support for affirmative action programs is related to race in America?

Now look at the effect that gender has on an individual's willingness to support affirmative action programs.

→ Data File: **SURVEY**
→ Task: **ANALYZE—DESCRIPTIVE STATISTICS—CROSSTABS**
→ Row Variable: **AFFRMACT**
→ Column Variable: **SEX**
→ View 1: **STATISTICS—PHI AND CRAMER'S V**
→ View 2: **CELLS—PERCENTAGE—COLUMN**

23. Before you try to determine whether there is a relationship, state a research and a null hypothesis for the relationship that you expect to find between the two variables.

Research Hypothesis:

Null Hypothesis:

After you examine the SPSSW output, write the column percentages in Table 6-4 and respond to the questions that follow.

Table 6-4 Support for Affirmative Action by Gender %

Support for Affirmative Action	Male	Female
Favor		
Oppose		

24. Compare the percentages horizontally and describe the pattern.

25. What is the value of the Cramer's V statistic for this relationship?

26. Is this relationship statistically significant?

Y N

27. Do you reject the null hypothesis?

Y N

28. Based on these results, what would you conclude about the extent to which support for affirmative action programs is related to gender in America?

29. Do these results surprise you? Why or why not?

6-3 Examining Linkage Institutions

6-3a Exercise Two

Linkage institutions are important to the American political process. Political parties, political interest groups, and the media are the conduits that deliver public demands to the institutions that process them. These linkage institutions also inform the public about policies and actions resulting from their original demands.

Recall from your textbook that political parties have several major functions such as proposing alternative government programs. Furthermore, there is a strong link between political ideology and political party affiliation. Republicans, for example, tend to see themselves as moderate to conservative. Democrats, on the other hand, tend to be moderate to liberal. This would suggest that Republicans would tend to support programs enhancing economic and social order, while Democrats would tend to support programs promoting equality.

Examine a policy question that demonstrates variation in party support.

→ Data File: SURVEY
→ Task: **ANALYZE—DESCRIPTIVE STATISTICS—CROSSTABS**
→ Row Variable: **ABORTANY**
→ Column Variable: **PARTY**
→ View 1: **STATISTICS—PHI AND CRAMER'S V**
→ View 2: **CELLS—PERCENTAGE—COLUMN**

Here the dependent variable, **ABORTANY,** measures public support for a woman seeking an abortion for any reason.

30. Before you try to determine whether there is a relationship, state a research and a null hypothesis for the relationship that you expect to find between the two variables.

Research Hypothesis:

Null Hypothesis:

After you examine the SPSSW output, write the column percentages in Table 6-5 and respond to the questions that follow.

Table 6-5 Support for Abortion for Any Reason by Political Party Affiliation %

Support for Abortion for Any Reason	Democrats	Independents	Republicans
Yes			
No			

31. Compare the percentages horizontally and describe the pattern.

32. What is the value of the Cramer's V statistic for this relationship?

33. Is this relationship statistically significant?

Y N

34. Do you reject the null hypothesis?

Y N

35. Which party affiliation is the most supportive of a woman's right to choose an abortion for any reason?

Democrat **Independent** **Republican**

36. Which party affiliation is the least supportive of a woman's right to choose an abortion for any reason?

Democrat **Independent** **Republican**

37. What do the results suggest about the relationship between political party and support for a woman seeking an abortion for any reason?

"All I know is what I read in the papers." Although Will Rogers probably said this with irony, many Americans may believe this. One can infer from the statement that the media is a very important agent of political socialization because it is a source of information about politics for many Americans. Election campaigns, for example, are major media events. While candidates attempt to personally meet the electorate, few Americans really get to see them in person. Thus, much of the voting public relies on the media to obtain information about candidates. Look at the extent of media use by the public to obtain information about the views and backgrounds of political candidates.

→ Data File: **SURVEY**
→ Task: **ANALYZE—DESCRIPTIVE STATISTICS—FREQUENCIES**
→ Variable 1: **POLPAPER**
→ Variable 2: **POLMAG1**
→ Variable 3: **POLMAG2**
→ Variable 4: **POLTV**
→ Variable 5: **MEDIAUSE**
→ View 1: **FREQUENCIES**
→ View 2: **STATISTICS—MEAN—MEDIAN—MODE**

Note: The above SPSSW Guide will simultaneously produce a frequency table for each of the variables.

The variables in this SPSSW Guide measure the extent to which the public uses newspapers, general magazines (*Time*), specialty magazines (*Mother Jones*), and television to obtain information about political campaigns. The **MEDIAUSE** variable is an index that measures the extent to which the public uses a variety of media sources to obtain political information. A value of 4 indicates that a respondent uses each of the forms of media to obtain political information. When you are familiar with the frequency distributions, fill in Table 6-6 and answer the questions that follow.

38. What is the level of measurement for each of the variables? (Circle the correct response)

POLPAPER	Nominal	Ordinal	Interval	Ratio
POLMAG1	Nominal	Ordinal	Interval	Ratio
POLMAG2	Nominal	Ordinal	Interval	Ratio
POLTV	Nominal	Ordinal	Interval	Ratio
MEDIAUSE	Nominal	Ordinal	Interval	Ratio

Table 6-6 Use of the Media to Obtain Information about a Political Candidate's Views/Background (Yes)

Media Source	Number	Valid Percent
Newspapers		
General Magazines		
Specialty Magazines		
Television		

39. Which of the individual forms of media do the respondents use the most?

40. Which of the individual forms of media do the respondents use the least?

41. What is the value of the appropriate measure of central tendency to use with the **POLPAPER** variable?

42. What is the value of the appropriate measure of central tendency to use with the **MEDIAUSE** variable?

43. Based on these results, what can you conclude about Americans' use of the media to obtain information about political candidates?

In 1993, many Americans watched in horror as an American soldier was dragged through the streets of Mogadishu, Somalia. As a result, the American public strongly demanded that American troops be removed from Somalia. President Clinton was also moved by what he saw on television and, as a result, removed American troops six months later.

On September 11, 2001, millions of Americans were once again horrified as they watched hijacked passenger planes crash into the World Trade Center and the Pentagon. The public's outcry provided the justification for President Bush to confidently declare the war on terror. It also allowed Congress to initiate action that would, in many ways, limit some freedoms Americans have taken for granted.

The media is important to the American political system. Not only does it inform citizens about political issues and candidates, it also brings world events to their living rooms in real time, via satellite. As discussed above, the public is very influenced by what they see. The public is so influenced, in fact, that it demands and expects action from political leaders. Thus, one would expect Americans to have some confidence in the media. After all, if confidence was low, would Americans have reacted so strongly to the telecasts from Somalia, New York, and Washington, DC? Examine the confidence Americans have in their media outlets.

→ Data File: **SURVEY**
→ Task: **ANALYZE—DESCRIPTIVE STATISTICS—FREQUENCIES**
→ Variable 1: **PRESS**
→ Variable 2: **TV**
→ Variable 3: **MEDIACON**
→ View 1: **FREQUENCIES**
→ View 2: **STATISTICS—MEAN—MEDIAN—MODE**

The **MEDIACON** variable is an index that measures the extent of the public's confidence in the media. When you are familiar with the frequency distribution, answer the following questions.

44. What is the level of measurement for each of the variables? (Circle the correct response)

PRESS	**Nominal**	**Ordinal**	**Interval**	**Ratio**
TV	**Nominal**	**Ordinal**	**Interval**	**Ratio**
MEDIACON	**Nominal**	**Ordinal**	**Interval**	**Ratio**

45. Is there much difference in the level of confidence the public has in the individual forms of media (PRESS and TV)?

Y **N**

46. What is the value of the appropriate measure of central tendency to use with the **MEDIACON** variable?

47. Based on these results, what do you conclude about the level of confidence Americans have in the media?

Why do some Americans have more confidence in the media than other Americans? For years liberal social critics have denounced members of the press for selecting news events that augment the economic values of the establishment at the expense of socialist viewpoints. On the other hand, conservatives assert that the media pay more attention to the foes of traditional values.

See to what extent political ideology answers this research question.

→ Data File: SURVEY
→ Task: ANALYZE—DESCRIPTIVE STATISTICS—CROSSTABS
→ Row Variable: MEDIACON
→ Column Variable: POLVIEW
→ View 1: STATISTICS—PHI AND CRAMER'S V
→ View 2: CELLS—PERCENTAGE—COLUMN

48. Before you try to determine whether there is a relationship, state a research and a null hypothesis for the relationship that you expect to find between the two variables.

Research Hypothesis:

Null Hypothesis:

After you examine the SPSSW output, write the column percentages in Table 6-7 and respond to the questions that follow.

Table 6-7 Confidence in the Media by Political Ideology %

Level of Confidence	Liberal	Moderate	Conservative
None			
Some			
Much			

49. Compare the percentages horizontally and describe the pattern.

50. What is the value of the Cramer's V statistic for this relationship?

51. Is this relationship statistically significant?

Y N

52. Do you reject the null hypothesis?

Y N

53. Which group has the most confidence in the media?

Liberal **Moderate** **Conservative**

54. Which group has the least confidence in the media?

Liberal **Moderate** **Conservative**

55. What do the results suggest about the relationship between political ideology and confidence in the media?

6-4 Examining the Decision-Making Institutions of American Government

Now turn your attention to the decision-making institutions of the United States government. In the following sections you will examine the workings of Congress, the presidency and the federal courts.

6-4a Exercise Three: The Congress

The United States Congress is the chief lawmaking institution in the American political system. The framers of the Constitution intended Congress to be the most powerful decision-making institution in the federal government. As such, many congressional scholars try to answer the following question: What factors influence the vote of a member of Congress?

Some argue that political party leaders in each chamber exert considerable influence on the members. Others believe that public interest groups have substantial influence in Congress because they provide members with the resources necessary for their campaigns. They also provide valuable information to aid members in the legislative process. The opinions of a legislator's constituency can also influence a congressional member. After all, legislators were elected to represent the people. In addition, the President plays an important role in the lawmaking process. The President is the *chief legislator.* Consequently, Congress is very reactive to many of the President's proposals.

Examine a phenomenon that deals with this question: party unity voting. Party unity votes are those in which a majority of one party votes one way and a majority of the other party votes the opposite way. In a true majoritarian system, parties will vote against each other on the key issues.

→ Data File: **SENATE**
→ Task: **ANALYZE—DESCRIPTIVE STATISTICS—CROSSTABS**
→ Row Variable: **ASHCROFT**
→ Column Variable: **PARTY**
→ View 1: **STATISTICS—PHI AND CRAMER'S V—LAMBDA**
→ View 2: **CELLS—PERCENTAGE—COLUMN**

Note: A sample will not be used in this exercise; the entire population of the U.S. Senate is available. Therefore, questions dealing with statistical significance will be skipped to concentrate on the strength of the relationship.

The dependent variable, **ASHCROFT,** deals with the confirmation of President Bush's nomination of John Ashcroft to be the attorney general. Ashcroft's nomination was controversial because of his beliefs about issues such as abortion, capital punishment, and prayer in public schools. Based on the readings and exercises you have completed thus far, which political party do you think would be most supportive of his confirmation?

Democratic **Republican** **Independent**

56. Before you try to determine whether there is a relationship, state a research and a null hypothesis for the relationship that you expect to find between the two variables.

Research Hypothesis:

Null Hypothesis:

After you examine the SPSSW output, write the column percentages in Table 6-8 and respond to the questions that follow.

Table 6-8 Ashcroft Confirmation Vote by Political Party %

Vote	*Democratic*	*Republican*	*Independent*
Yea			
Nay			

57. Compare the percentages horizontally and describe the pattern.

58. What is the value of the Cramer's V statistic for this relationship?

59. Which party had the most support for Ashcroft?

Democratic **Republican** **Independent**

60. Give a proportional reduction of error (PRE) interpretation of these results.

61. Is your original hypothesis correct?

Y **N**

62. Does this vote appear to be a party unity vote?

Y **N**

63. What do the results suggest about the relationship between political party and the Ashcroft confirmation vote?

The American Conservative Union (ACU) is a conservative interest group that is active in congressional lobbying. The ACU is supportive of capitalism, believes in the doctrine of the original intent of the Constitution's framers, and stresses support for traditional moral values. Since 1971, the ACU has rated each member of Congress on a scale of 0 to 100. The scale is based on the votes cast on a variety of issues. The ratings are designed to gauge a representative's adherence to the above principles.

The ACU influences congressional members the same ways that other interest groups influence Congress. The ACU, for example, contributes financial support to the candidates that support their views. Conservative members of Congress also use the ratings to show their constituencies that they are supporting conservative values. Liberal members, on the other hand, use the ratings to convince their constituencies that they are not supporting conservative values. In short, the ACU provides the political resources discussed in Chapter 5 of the textbook.

During the 107th session of Congress, the ACU was very supportive of an education bill amendment that would allow federal education funds to be withheld from public schools that did not allow the Boy Scouts of America (BSA) to use school facilities. This amendment was proposed by Senator Jesse Helms (R-NC) in response to the BSA's policy toward gays. See if the ACU's lobbying efforts were effective.

→ Data File: **SENATE**
→ Task: **ANALYZE—DESCRIPTIVE STATISTICS—CROSSTABS**
→ Row Variable: **BSA**
→ Column Variable: **ACUCOLL**
→ View 1: **STATISTICS—PHI AND CRAMER'S V**
→ View 2: **CELLS—PERCENTAGE—COLUMN**

64. Before you try to determine whether there is a relationship, state a research and a null hypothesis for the relationship that you expect to find between the two variables.

Research Hypothesis:

Null Hypothesis:

After you examine the SPSSW output, write the column percentages in Table 6-9 and respond to the questions that follow.

Table 6-9 BSA Amendment Vote by ACU Rating %

Vote	*Very Low*	*Low*	*High*	*Very High*
Yea				
Nay				

65. Compare the percentages horizontally and describe the pattern.

66. What is the value of the Cramer's V statistic for this relationship?

67. Which category had the most support for the amendment?

Very Low **Low** **High** **Very High**

68. Is your original hypothesis correct?

Y **N**

69. Did the amendment pass?

Y **N**

70. What do the results suggest about the relationship between the ACU's efforts and the BSA amendment vote?

President Bush declared during his campaign that he wanted to be known as the "Education President." One of his proposals was to implement a school voucher program that would allow public school children to use federal funds (vouchers) to transfer to another public school or another private school. See if President Bush was successful in his role as the chief legislator and at the same time examine party influence on the vote.

→ Data File: **SENATE**
→ Task: **ANALYZE—DESCRIPTIVE STATISTICS—CROSSTABS**
→ Row Variable: **VOUCHERS**
→ Column Variable: **PARTY**
→ View 1: **STATISTICS—PHI AND CRAMER'S V**
→ View 2: **CELLS—PERCENTAGE—COLUMN**

Based on the readings and exercises you have completed thus far, which political party do you think would be most supportive of his confirmation?

Democratic **Republican** **Independent**

Before you try to determine whether there is a relationship, state a research and a null hypothesis for the relationship that you expect to find between the two variables.

Research Hypothesis:

Null Hypothesis:

After you examine the SPSSW output, write the column percentages in Table 6-10 and respond to the questions that follow.

Table 6-10 Support for Voucher Amendment by Political Party %

Vote	*Democratic*	*Republican*	*Independent*
Did Not Vote			
Yea			
Nay			

71. Compare the percentages horizontally and describe the pattern.

72. What is the value of the Cramer's V statistic for this relationship?

73. Which party had the most support for the school voucher program?

Democratic **Republican** **Independent**

74. Is your original hypothesis correct?

Y N

75. Does this vote appear to be a party unity vote?

Y N

76. Did the amendment pass?

Y N

77. What do these results suggest about the president's persuasive power in Congress?

78. What do the results suggest about the relationship between political party affiliation and support for the voucher program?

6-4b Exercise Four: The Presidency

Presidential scholars have identified several sources of presidential power: the U.S. Constitution, precedents established by predecessors, and congressional legislation. In the following exercises, you will concentrate on the Constitution as a power source.

Article I of the Constitution provides a comprehensive list of congressional powers. On the other hand, Article II is far less detailed in prescribing presidential powers. Nonetheless, scholars have categorized presidential powers into five functional areas. As *chief executive,* the executive power of the nation is vested in the President. Thus, he is responsible for ensuring that the laws are faithfully executed. To assist him in fulfilling this role, the President can make appointments to executive positions. In addition, while not specified in the Constitution, presidents can issue executive orders to federal agencies. President Truman, for example, integrated the armed forces with an executive order. Examine the extent to which presidents have used executive orders.

→ Data File: **PRESIDENTS**
→ Task: **ANALYZE—DESCRIPTIVE STATISTICS—FREQUENCIES**
→ Variable: **EXECORD**
→ View 1: **FREQUENCIES**
→ View 2: **STATISTICS—MEAN—MEDIAN—MODE—STD. DEVIATION—VARIANCE—MINIMUM—MAXIMUM**

After you have reviewed the SPSSW output, respond to the following questions.

79. What was the mean number of executive orders issued by the presidents?

80. What was the median number of executive orders issued by the presidents?

81. Which of the measures of central tendency is the most appropriate to use?

Mode **Median** **Mean**

82. What was the minimum and maximum number of executive orders issued by the presidents?

Minimum ___________
Maximum ___________

83. What is the value of the standard deviation for the number of executive orders issued by the presidents?

84. What is the value of the variance for the number of executive orders issued by the presidents?

85. Succinctly interpret the standard deviation.

As *chief diplomat,* the President makes international treaties, appoints ambassadors, and receives foreign ambassadors. Although not covered in the Constitution, presidents also negotiate executive agreements with the heads of other nations. Examine the extent to which presidents have entered into international treaties and executive agreements.

→ Data File: **PRESIDENTS**
→ Task: **ANALYZE—DESCRIPTIVE STATISTICS—FREQUENCIES**
→ Variable 1: **TREATIES**
→ Variable 2: **EXECAGR**
→ View 1: **FREQUENCIES**
→ View 2: **STATISTICS—MEAN—MEDIAN—MODE—STD. DEVIATION—VARIANCE—MINIMUM—MAXIMUM**

After you have reviewed the SPSSW output, fill in Table 6-11 and respond to the questions that follow.

Table 6-11 The President as Chief Diplomat

Variable	Mean	Median	Std. Dev	Min	Max
TREATIES					
EXECAGR					

86. What was the mean number of executive agreements negotiated by the presidents?

87. What was the median number of treaties negotiated by the presidents?

88. Which of the measures of central tendency is the most appropriate to use with the variables?

Mode **Median** **Mean**

89. What was the maximum number of executive agreements negotiated by the presidents?

90. What was the minimum number of treaties negotiated by the presidents?

91. Succinctly interpret the standard deviation for each variable.

92. Which diplomatic tool did the presidents use the most?

93. Based on your readings, why have presidents used one diplomatic tool more than the other?

As *chief judge*, the President is empowered to appoint members to the federal judiciary. He also has the power to grant pardons and reprieves. Although there is some dispute, the presidential pardon is absolute. That is, once granted the Constitution does not provide a way to reverse a pardon nor is an authority identified who could issue a reversal. In addition, given the range of discretion provided by the Constitution, presidents have pardoned socialist leaders (Eugene Debs by Harding), former presidents (Nixon by Ford), and members of Congress (Dan Rostenkowski by Clinton). Other acts of clemency include amnesty to members of the Confederacy (Andrew Johnson) and Vietnam draft resisters (Carter). Examine the frequency to which presidents have used the power to grant pardons and reprieves.

→ Data File: **PRESIDENTS**
→ Task: **ANALYZE—DESCRIPTIVE STATISTICS—FREQUENCIES**
→ Variable 1: **CLEMENCY**
→ View 1: **FREQUENCIES**
→ View 2: **STATISTICS—MEAN—MEDIAN—MODE—STD. DEVIATION—VARIANCE—MINIMUM—MAXIMUM**

After you have reviewed the SPSSW output, respond to the following questions.

94. What was the mean number of clemency actions issued by the presidents?

95. What was the median number of clemency actions issued by the presidents?

96. Which of the measures of central tendency is the most appropriate to use?

Mode **Median** **Mean**

97. What was the minimum and maximum number of clemency actions issued by the presidents?

Minimum ___________
Maximum ___________

98. What is the value of the standard deviation for the number of clemency actions issued by the presidents?

99. What is the value of the variance for the number of clemency actions issued by the presidents?

100. Succinctly interpret the standard deviation.

The Constitution also gives the President some responsibilities relating to Congress. He can, for example, convene and adjourn Congress, sign or veto legislation, and he is required to deliver a periodic State of the Union Address to Congress. The President's role as *chief legislator* is so important that many presidential scholars measure presidential success in terms of the President's ability to persuade Congress to legislate presidential initiatives. A successful president can be seen as one who achieved many of his legislative initiatives. Thus, one way to examine his legislative success is to examine the number of vetoes a president used. After all, a veto suggests that a president is dissatisfied with congressional legislation. Examine the extent presidents have used the presidential veto.

→ Data File: **PRESIDENTS**
→ Task: **ANALYZE—DESCRIPTIVE STATISTICS—FREQUENCIES**
→ Variable 1: **PRESVETO**
→ View 1: **FREQUENCIES**
→ View 2: **STATISTICS—MEAN—MEDIAN—MODE—STD. DEVIATION—VARIANCE—MINIMUM—MAXIMUM**

After you have reviewed the SPSSW output, respond to the following questions.

101. What was the mean number of vetoes issued by the presidents?

102. What was the median number of vetoes issued by the presidents?

103. Which of the measures of central tendency is the most appropriate to use?

Mode **Median** **Mean**

104. What was the minimum and maximum number of vetoes issued by the presidents?

Minimum ___________
Maximum ___________

105. What is the value of the standard deviation for the number of vetoes issued by the presidents?

106. What is the value of the variance for the number of vetoes issued by the presidents?

107. Succinctly interpret the standard deviation.

In addition to the above formal roles, the President is also the *Commander-in-Chief* of the armed forces. Return to Chapter 2 of this workbook for an exercise that examines our presidents and their military careers.

Since 1948 when historian Arthur Schlesinger, Sr., asked fifty-five of his fellow historians to rate each president, several institutions have conducted surveys of presidential greatness. These surveys have become more complex, yet over the years the presidents judged as great (e.g., Lincoln) and those judged as failures (e.g., Harding) remain stable groups. The other presidents either move up (e.g., Eisenhower) or down the list (e.g., Kennedy). Critics contend that the survey's participants bias the rankings depending on which presidential biographers take part. Defining greatness is also difficult. Presidents who served during crises, however, are somewhat easier to rate. Survey participants, for example, have consistently considered Abraham Lincoln a great president because of his actions during the Civil War. On the other hand, those who immediately preceded and followed Lincoln in office are consistently ranked below average (e.g., Grant) or as failures (e.g., Pierce, Buchanan, Andrew Johnson).

Why do scholars rank the presidents as they do? Perhaps it has something to do with their approach to the presidency. After all, a president can be an active man. Some presidents, however, are more active than others. Abraham Lincoln, for example, was very active. He believed that he could take any action when the security of the nation was at stake. Consequently he even violated the Constitution at times in order to save the union. Other presidents, for example, William Howard Taft, asserted that presidents were restricted to the powers specified in the Constitution. Thus, as chief diplomat, presidents should negotiate treaties in lieu of executive agreements. Theodore Roosevelt, on the other hand, argued that presidents represent the nation, and should thus be stewards of the national interest. According to this view, presidents can take any action that is not explicitly prohibited by law or the Constitution.

Examine what effect presidential activity has on the rankings of U.S. Presidents. First, however, produce frequency tables for the variables and respond to the questions that follow.

→ Data File: **PRESIDENTS**
→ Task: **ANALYZE—DESCRIPTIVE STATISTICS—FREQUENCIES**
→ Variable 1: **COLRANK**
→ Variable 2: **ACTIVE**
→ View: **FREQUENCIES**

Note: You will not use a sample in this exercise; the entire population of U.S. Presidents is available. Therefore, questions dealing with statistical significance will be skipped to concentrate on the strength of the relationship.

108. What is the level of measurement for the **RANKCOL** variable?

Nominal **Ordinal** **Interval** **Ratio**

109. What is the level of measurement for the **ACTIVE** variable?

Nominal **Ordinal** **Interval** **Ratio**

110. What is the appropriate measure of association to use?

111. State a research and a null hypothesis for the relationship that you expect to find between the two variables.

Research Hypothesis:

Null Hypothesis:

Determine and fill in the appropriate statistics to use in View 1.

→ Data File: **PRESIDENT**
→ Task: **ANALYZE—DESCRIPTIVE STATISTICS—CROSSTABS**
→ Row Variable: **COLRANK**
→ Column Variable: **ACTIVE**
→ View 1: **STATISTICS—**____________________
→ View 2: **CELLS—PERCENTAGE—COLUMN**

Table 6-12 Presidential Rankings by Level of Presidential Activity %

Ranking	*Restrained*	*Active*	*Very Active*
Below Avg./Failure			
Avg./Above Avg.			
Great/Near Great			

After you examine the SPSSW output, write the column percentages in Table 6-12 and respond to the questions that follow.

112. Compare the percentages horizontally and describe the pattern.

113. What percentage of the great and near-great presidents were very active?

114. How many of the presidents judged below average and failures were very active?

115. What is the value of the appropriate measure of association for this relationship?

116. What is the PRE interpretation for the measure?

117. Even though you have the entire population, what might explain the level of significance for this relationship?

118. Is your original hypothesis correct?

Y N

119. What do these results suggest about presidential activity and subsequent rankings?

6-4c Exercise Five: The Judiciary

The Constitution specifies qualifications for individuals wishing to hold office in Congress or to serve as president or vice president. The document, however, is silent regarding qualifications to serve as a member of the federal judiciary. This leads to an interesting question: Are there informal qualifications to serve in the judiciary? Try to identify factors that characterize a *typical* U.S. Supreme Court justice.

→ Data File: **COURT**
→ Task: **ANALYZE—DESCRIPTIVE STATISTICS—FREQUENCIES**
→ Variable 1: **ATTENDLA**
→ Variable 2: **IVY**
→ Variable 3: **JUDICIAL**
→ Variable 4: **NJUDYRS**
→ Variable 5: **PIDLINK**
→ Variable 6: **RELIGION**
→ Variable 7: **REGION**
→ Variable 8: **PRIOREXP**
→ View 1: **FREQUENCIES**
→ View 2: **STATISTICS—MODE**

The first two variables deal with law school attendance (**ATTENDLA**) and the law school a justice attended (**IVY**). The **JUDICIAL** variable indicates whether a justice has prior judicial experience. The fourth variable (**NJUDYRS**) measures judicial experience. The **PIDLINK** variable measures the partisanship of the appointing president and the justice. The next two variables, **RELIGION** and **REGION,** measure the religious affiliation and the region of residence of a justice. The last variable **PRIOREXP** measures the predominant area of experience for a justice. Thus, while a justice may have worked mainly in the private sector, they may also have some legal/judicial experience.

When you are familiar with the individual frequency tables, fill in Table 6-13, and respond to the questions that follow.

Table 6-13 Characteristics of U.S. Supreme Court Justices

Variable	Modal Response	Modal Frequency	Modal Valid %
ATTENDLA	No	67	62.0
IVY			
JUDICIAL			
NJUDYRS			
PIDLINK			
RELIGION			
REGION			
PRIOREXP			

120. What is the predominant characteristic of the justices?

121. What is the least predominant characteristic of the justices?

122. Which characteristic has the most variation in the distribution?

123. Which characteristic has the least variation in the distribution?

124. What percentage of the justices are not *Protestant/Other?*

125. How many justices are from the West Coast?

126. Does law school attendance seem to be an informal qualification?

Y N

127. Does the data suggest a linkage between a president and appointee?

Y N

128. Do these preliminary results suggest that there are some informal qualifications to be a justice on the U.S. Supreme Court?

Y N

129. Succinctly describe a *typical* Supreme Court justice.

Are you surprised by some of the frequency results? Did you, for example, expect to find more justices who attended law school than the results reflect? Also, did you expect to find that most of the justices had some judicial experience? After all, you have read that legal and judicial experiences are important considerations. See if these attributes are more important today than they were in the earlier years of the republic.

130. What is the level of measurement for the **JUDICIAL** variable?

Nominal **Ordinal** **Interval** **Ratio**

131. What is the level of measurement for the ERA variable?

Nominal **Ordinal** **Interval** **Ratio**

132. What is the appropriate measure of association to use?

133. State a research and a null hypothesis for the relationship that you expect to find between the two variables.

Research Hypothesis:

Null Hypothesis:

Determine and fill in the appropriate statistics to use in View 1.

→ Data File: **COURT**
→ Task: **ANALYZE—DESCRIPTIVE STATISTICS—CROSSTABS**
→ Row Variable: **JUDICIAL**
→ Column Variable: **ERA**
→ View 1: **STATISTICS—__________________**
→ View 2: **CELLS—PERCENTAGE—COLUMN**

Note: You will not use a sample in this exercise; the entire population of U.S. Supreme Court members is available. Therefore, questions dealing with statistical significance will be skipped to concentrate on the strength of the relationship.

After you examine the SPSSW output, write the column percentages in Table 6-14 and respond to the questions that follow.

Table **6-14 Judicial Experience by Era of Service %**

Judicial Experience	*19th Century*	*Pre-Warren Court*	*Post-Warren Court*
Yes			
No			

134. Compare the percentages horizontally and describe the pattern.

135. What percentage of the 19th-century justices had judicial experience?

136. How many of the Post-Warren justices did not have judicial experience?

137. What is the value of the appropriate measure of association for this relationship?

138. Even though you have the entire population, what might explain the level of significance for this relationship?

139. Is your original hypothesis correct?

Y N

140. What do these results suggest about a justice's era of service and judicial experience?

Now see if there is a relationship between the era of service and whether a justice attended law school.

→ Data File: **COURT**
→ Task: **ANALYZE—DESCRIPTIVE STATISTICS—CROSSTABS**
→ Row Variable: **ATTENDLA**
→ Column Variable: **ERA**
→ View 1: **STATISTICS—PHI AND CRAMER'S V—LAMBDA**
→ View 2: **CELLS—PERCENTAGE—COLUMN**

State a research and a null hypothesis for the relationship that you expect to find between the two variables.

Research Hypothesis:

Null Hypothesis:

After you examine the SPSSW output, write the column percentages in Table 6-15 and respond to the questions that follow.

Table 6-15 Attend Law School by Era of Service %

Law School	*19th Century*	*Pre-Warren Court*	*Post-Warren Court*
Yes			
No			

141. Compare the percentages horizontally and describe the pattern.

142. What percentage of the 19th-century justices attended law school?

143. How many of the Post-Warren justices did not attend law school?

144. What is the value of the appropriate measure of association for this relationship?

145. What is the PRE interpretation for the relationship?

146. Even though you have the entire population, what might explain the level of significance for this relationship?

147. Is your original hypothesis correct?

Y **N**

148. What do these results suggest about a justice's era of service and law school attendance?

Now examine the effect that era of service has on the prior experience of a justice.

→ Data File: **COURT**
→ Task: **ANALYZE—DESCRIPTIVE STATISTICS—CROSSTABS**
→ Row Variable: **PRIOREXP**
→ Column Variable: **ERA**
→ View 1: **STATISTICS—PHI AND CRAMER'S V**
→ View 2: **CELLS—PERCENTAGE—COLUMN**

State a research and a null hypothesis for the relationship that you expect to find between the two variables.

Research Hypothesis:

Null Hypothesis:

After you examine the SPSSW output, write the column percentages in Table 6-16 and respond to the following questions that follow.

Table 6-16 Prior Experience by Era of Service %

Prior Experience	*19th Century*	*Pre-Warren Court*	*Post-Warren Court*
Private Legal			
State Judicial			
Federal Judicial			
Federal Non-judicial			
State Non-judicial			
Private Non-legal			

149. Compare the percentages horizontally and describe the pattern.

150. What percentage of the 19th-century justices had judicial experience?

151. How many of the Post-Warren justices worked in the executive or legislative branches of the federal government prior to their appointment to the Supreme Court?

152. What is the value of the Cramer's V statistic for this relationship?

153. What is the PRE interpretation for the relationship?

154. Is your original hypothesis correct?

Y N

155. What do these results suggest about a justice's era of service and experience?

Chapter Quiz

1. At times, the American government has taken steps to limit certain types of speech in an effort to perform its duty to
a. promote freedom.
b. maintain order.
c. enhance equality.
d. protect minority groups.

Use Table 6-17 to respond to Questions 2 and 3. The table depicts the relationship between tolerance for divisive forms of speech and race.

Table 6-17 Tolerance toward Divisive Forms of Speech by Race %

Level of Support	*White*	*African American*
Very low	38.4	45.4
Low	6.8	10.9
High	24.2	23.6
Very high	30.6	20.1
Total	2238	432

2. The table suggests
a. African Americans are more supportive of divisive forms of speech than whites.
b. whites are more supportive of divisive forms of speech than African Americans.
c. there is no difference in the level of support for divisive forms of speech for the two racial groups.
d. there is a substantial relationship between the variables.

3. ___ is the appropriate measure of association to use with Table 6-17.
a. Phi
b. Cramer's V
c. Gamma
d. Tau b

4. Table 6-18 depicts the extent of confidence Americans have in the media.

Table 6-18 Extent of Confidence in the Media

Category	Frequency	Percentage
None	474	25.3
Sometimes	662	35.3
Much	737	39.4

What is the value of the modal response?

a. None
b. Sometimes
c. Much
d. 737

Table 6-19 depicts the party affiliation of America's presidents.

Table 6-19 Political Party of American Presidents

Category	Frequency	Percentage
Democrat Republican	4	9.3
Whig	4	9.3
Democratic	14	32.5
Republican	18	41.9
Other	3	7.0

5. What percentage of America's presidents did not belong to one of the current major parties?
   a. 7.0
   b. 9.3
   c. 18.6
   d. 25.6

Use Table 6-20 to respond to Questions 6 and 7. The table depicts the relationship between political party and military service for America's presidents.

Table 6-20 President's Military Service by Political Party

Military Service	*Democratic*	*Republican*	*Other*
Yes	50.0	66.7	45.5
No	50.0	33.3	54.5
Total	14	18	11

6. The table suggests there is
   a. a weak relationship between the variables.
   b. a moderate relationship between the variables.
   c. a strong relationship between the variables.
   d. no relationship between the variables.
7. The ___ statistic is the appropriate measure of association to use with the table.
   a. Phi
   b. Cramer's V
   c. Lambda
   d. Tau-c

Use Table 6-21 to respond to Questions 8, 9, and 10. The table depicts the relationship between a U.S. Senator's support for school vouchers and the Senator's rating by the American Conservative Union (ACU).

Table 6-21 Support for School Vouchers by ACU Rating

Vote	*Very Low*	*Low*	*High*	*Very High*
Yes	0.0	11.5	60.0	92.0
No	100.0	88.5	40.0	8.0
Total	23	26	25	25

8. The table suggests there is
   a. a weak relationship between the variables.
   b. a moderate relationship between the variables.
   c. a strong relationship between the variables.
   d. no relationship between the variables.
9. The ___ statistic is the appropriate measure of association to use with the table.
   a. Phi
   b. Cramer's V
   c. Lambda
   d. Tau-c

   The following statistics were produced for the table
   - Cramer's V: 0.75
   - Pearson contingency coefficient (C): 0.60
   - Lambda: 0.63
   - Tau c: –0.81
10. What is the value of the appropriate statistic?
    a. 0.75
    b. 0.60
    c. .63
    d. –.81

Chapter 7

Public Administration and Public Policy

Outline

7-1 Introduction

Toward the end of the nineteenth century political scientists began to look at public administration as a professional field of study. Scholars debated the *politics-administration* dichotomy, examined the administrative structure, studied the decision- and budget-making processes, analyzed the interaction between public managers and their subordinates, and delved into administrative accountability and ethics. Today, many universities award graduate degrees in Public Administration. Consequently, public administration has proven to be a fertile field for research. In this workbook chapter you will examine questions dealing with the public's attitude toward the administrative sector. Before you start working on the exercises in this chapter, you should have a thorough understanding of Chapter 6 in the textbook.

7-2 Examining Public Support for Government Spending

7-2a Exercise One

The U.S. Constitution says very little about the federal bureaucracy. Yet today this bureaucracy, in some way, affects all citizens and is a source of direct and indirect employment for millions of Americans. In addition, it seems that every time someone says "there ought to be a law," the size and impact of the bureaucracy expands. At the same time Americans are critical of government because they believe that it is too intrusive, has become too powerful, and wastes tax dollars. When asked about specific programs, however, they tend to be much more supportive of their government. Millions of Americans, for example, enjoy a better quality of life because of government social programs. Others feel more secure because of attempts to combat crime and ensure a strong military presence throughout the world. Examine the level of support Americans have for government spending.

→ Data File: **SURVEY**
→ Task: **ANALYZE—DESCRIPTIVE STATISTICS—FREQUENCIES**
→ Variable 1: **ENVIRON**
→ Variable 2: **HEALTH**
→ Variable 3: **CRIME**
→ Variable 4: **DRUGS**
→ Variable 5: **EDUCATE**
→ Variable 6: **BLACK**
→ Variable 7: **DEFENSE**
→ Variable 8: **FORAID**
→ Variable 9: **WELFARE**
→ View 1: **FREQUENCIES**
→ View 2: **STATISTICS—MODE**

After you are familiar with the individual frequency tables, fill in Table 7-1 and respond to the questions that follow.

1. Which is the *best* category to reflect the public's acceptance for government spending on a particular program?

TOO LITTLE **RIGHT** **TOO MUCH**

Table 7-1 Public Support for Governmental Spending

Variable	Modal Response	Modal Frequency	Modal Valid %
ENVIRON			
HEALTH			
CRIME			
DRUGS			
EDUCATE			
BLACK			
DEFENSE			
FORAID			
WELFARE			

2. Based on your readings, which programs deal with the maintenance of order as a government responsibility?

3. Based on your readings, which programs deal with the provision of public goods and services as a government responsibility?

4. Based on your readings, which programs deal with the promotion of equality as a government responsibility?

5. Which program does the public believe to be the most underfunded?

6. Which program does the public believe to be the most overfunded?

7. Based on these results, which program has the most variation in its level of support?

8. Based on these results, which two programs would be the most difficult for politicians to trim? Explain and defend your answer.

9. In your opinion, which program has the greatest risk of having its funding trimmed? Explain and defend your answer.

7-3 Examining Public Support for Defense Spending

7-3a Exercise Two

National defense has been the centerpiece of American foreign policy for many years. In addition, following the terrorist attacks against the World Trade Center and the Pentagon, President Bush has made it clear that the war against terror will be the crux of future American foreign policy. The first exercise in this chapter examined the level of support Americans have toward defense spending. Now identify some of the program's major supporters.

The following SPSSW Guide will allow you to run simultaneous cross tabs and generate the appropriate measures of association for several nominal independent variables.

→ Data File:	**SURVEY**
→ Task:	**ANALYZE—DESCRIPTIVE STATISTICS—CROSSTABS**
→ Row Variable:	**DEFENSE**
→ Column Variable 1:	**SEX**
→ Column Variable 2:	**RACE**
→ Column Variable 3:	**PARTY**
→ Column Variable 4:	**POLVIEW**
→ View 1:	**STATISTICS—PHI AND CRAMER'S V**
→ View 2:	**CELLS—PERCENTAGE—COLUMN**

The following SPSSW Guide will allow you to run simultaneous cross tabs and generate the appropriate measures of association for two ordinal independent variables.

→ Data File:	**SURVEY**
→ Task:	**ANALYZE—DESCRIPTIVE STATISTICS—CROSSTABS**
→ Row Variable:	**DEFENSE**
→ Column Variable 5:	**FRTERROR**
→ Column Variable 6:	**NUCLRWAR**
→ View 1:	**STATISTICS—KENDALL'S TAU B**
→ View 2:	**CELLS—PERCENTAGE—COLUMN**

After you have reviewed the results, fill in Table 7-2. Then, use the results and the table to respond to the questions that follow.

Table 7-2 Support for Defense Spending (Level of Current Spending: Too Little)

Variable	Modal Group	% Support	Measure	Significance
SEX				
RACE				
PARTY				
POLVIEW				
FRTERROR				
NUCLRWAR				

10. Are all of the relationships statistically significant?

Y **N**

11. If you answered *no* to Question 10, which independent variable does not help explain the level of support for defense spending?

If you answered *yes* to question 10, circle:

Not Applicable

12. Which group would be the strongest advocate to increase defense spending?

13. Give a PRE interpretation for the relationship between **NUCLRWAR** and support for defense spending.

14. Succinctly describe the *typical* supporter of increased defense spending.

7-4 Examining the Federal Government's Obligation to the People

7-4a Exercise Three

For centuries societies have argued about the reasons for the existence of government. Even those who believe that government should be minimal have visualized the need for government to maintain order. To these individuals, the purpose of government is to deal with conflict. You may remember that Thomas Hobbes asserted that man was selfish and life without government would lead to an existence that was "solitary, poor, nasty, brutish and short." Others believe that the government should provide essential goods and services, such as public education. Later social agendas led to the government's role in the promotion of equality. These beliefs about the proper role of government are the basis for arguments about the need for, and the role of, government.

The promotion of equality, as a function of government, has sparked intense debate over the years. Some believe that the government is important in this role. Others, however, assert that individuals must make the effort to improve themselves without relying on the government. Still, others see government and the people working together to improve their lot in life. Examine the public's attitude toward government assistance to the poor.

→ Data File: **SURVEY**
→ Task: **ANALYZE—DESCRIPTIVE STATISTICS—FREQUENCIES**
→ Variable: **AIDPOOR**
→ View 1: **FREQUENCIES**
→ View 2: **STATISTICS—MODE**

When you are familiar with the SPSS output, respond to the following questions.

15. What is the modal category?

16. How many respondents believe that there should be cooperation between the government and the people in addressing poverty?

17. What percentage of the respondents believes that the people should take care of themselves?

18. Briefly describe the distribution of public opinion for this question.

As you can see from the above results, there is some dissension about the government's role in helping the poor. Identify those groups that see a major role for the government in this area.

→ Data File: SURVEY
→ Task: ANALYZE—DESCRIPTIVE STATISTICS—CROSSTABS
→ Row Variable: AIDPOOR
→ Column Variable 1: SEX
→ Column Variable 2: RACE
→ Column Variable 3: PARTY
→ Column Variable 4: RELIGION
→ Column Variable 5: POLVIEW
→ View 1: STATISTICS—PHI AND CRAMER'S V
→ View 2: CELLS—PERCENTAGE—COLUMN

After you have reviewed the results, fill in Table 7-3. Then, use the results and the table to respond to the questions that follow.

Table 7-3 Attitude toward Helping the Poor (Sole Responsibility of the Government)

Variable	Modal Group	% Support	Measure	Significance
SEX				
RACE				
PARTY				
RELIGION				
POLYVIEW				

19. Are all of the relationships statistically significant?

Y N

20. If you answered *no* to Question 19, which independent variable does not help explain the level of support for defense spending?

If you answered *yes* to Question 19, circle:

Not Applicable

21. Which group is the strongest advocate for having the government help the poor?

22. Which group is the strongest advocate for an alternative other than government to help the poor?

23. Succinctly describe the *typical* supporter of government assistance to the poor.

7-5 Examining the Public's Confidence in Government

7-5a Exercise Four

Public confidence in the federal government has seriously waned since the 1960's. Why? Several factors possibly account for the deterioration in confidence. First, the American public became very disenchanted with the government's handling of the war in Vietnam. Second, the social programs initiated by the Johnson administration expanded an already debatable role for government: the promotion of economic and social equity. Third, the unconstitutional acts prevalent during the Nixon years contributed to dissatisfaction throughout the country. Fourth, increases in the overall crime rate and violent crime rates in particular contributed to the notion that the government could not maintain order. Last, the unethical actions of politicians over the last three decades tainted their images and increased the decline in public confidence. In summary, Americans did not accept many actions of the federal government as lawful, fair, or just. Thus, questions concerning the legitimacy of the federal government existed.

Was the public's lack of confidence directed against specific institutions? Or did the public lose confidence in the government in general? Examine the public's confidence in the federal government by examining three separate institutions: the executive branch, the judiciary, and Congress.

→ Data File: **SURVEY**
→ Task: **ANALYZE—DESCRIPTIVE STATISTICS—FREQUENCIES**
→ Variable 1: **EXECBR**
→ Variable 2: **SUPCOURT**
→ Variable 3: **CONGRESS**
→ View 1: **FREQUENCIES**
→ View 2: **STATISTICS—MODE**

When you are familiar with the individual frequency tables, fill in Table 7-4 and respond to the questions that follow.

Table 7-4 Confidence in the Federal Government (Great Deal/Only Some)

Variable	Great Deal [#]	Only Some [#]	Great Deal [Valid %]	Only Some [Valid %]	Cumulative Percentage
EXECBR					
SUPCOURT					
CONGRESS					

24. Based on your readings, which federal institution did you expect the public to have the most confidence in? Circle one.

Executive **Supreme Court** **Congress**

25. Based on your readings, which federal institution did you expect the public to have the least confidence in? Circle one.

Executive **Supreme Court** **Congress**

26. Which institution does the public have the most confidence in? Circle one.

Executive **Supreme Court** **Congress**

27. Which institution does the public have the least confidence in? Circle one.

Executive **Supreme Court** **Congress**

28. Based on these results which institution has the most variation in its level of support? Circle one.

Executive **Supreme Court** **Congress**

29. Based on these results which institution has the least variation in its level of support? Circle one.

Executive **Supreme Court** **Congress**

Now examine the effect that political party affiliation has on the public's confidence in the executive branch of the federal government.

→ Data File: **SURVEY**
→ Task: **ANALYZE—DESCRIPTIVE STATISTICS—CROSSTABS**
→ Row Variable: **EXECBR**
→ Column Variable 1: **PARTY**
→ View 1: **STATISTICS—PHI AND CRAMER'S V**
→ View 2: **CELLS—PERCENTAGE—COLUMN**

30. Before you try to determine whether there is a relationship, state a research and a null hypothesis for the relationship that you expect to find between the two variables.

Research Hypothesis:

Null Hypothesis:

After you examine the SPSSW output respond to the questions that follow.

31. Compare the percentages horizontally and describe the pattern.

32. What is the value of the Cramer's V statistic for this relationship?

33. Is this relationship statistically significant?

Y **N**

34. Do you reject the null hypothesis?

Y **N**

35. Based on these results, describe the relationship between the two variables.

Now see how geography affects the original relationship.

→ Data File: **SURVEY**
→ Task: **ANALYZE—DESCRIPTIVE STATISTICS—CROSSTABS**
→ Row Variable: **EXECBR**
→ Column Variable 1: **PARTY**
→ Control Variable: **REGION**
→ View 1: **STATISTICS—PHI AND CRAMER'S V**
→ View 2: **CELLS—PERCENTAGE—COLUMN**

After you examine the SPSSW output, fill in Table 7-5 and respond to the questions that follow.

Table 7-5 Relationship between Confidence in the Executive Branch and Political Party by Region of the Country (Great Deal/Only Some)

Table	Demo.	Ind.	Repub.	V	Prob	Ho	Decision
Original							
East							
Midwest							
South							
West							

Use the following key to fill in the table cells.

Ho: A = Accept Null R = Reject Null
Decision: 1 = The original relationship is non-spurious
2 = The original relationship is spurious
3 = There is interaction

36. Which political party affiliation has the most confidence in the executive branch? Circle one.

Democrat Independent Republican

37. Which political party affiliation has the least confidence in the executive branch? Circle one.

Democrat Independent Republican

38. In which region of the country is Democrat confidence the lowest? Circle one.

East **Midwest** **South** **West**

39. In which region of the country is Republican confidence the highest? Circle one.

East **Midwest** **South** **West**

40. Summarize the effect that the control variable has on the original relationship.

Chapter Quiz

Use Table 7-6 to respond to Questions 1, 2, and 3. The table depicts the public's attitude toward government spending to improve the conditions of African Americans.

Table 7-6 Attitude toward Spending to Improve the Conditions of African Americans

Attitude	Frequencies	Percentage
Too little	469	37.9
Just right	563	45.6
Too much	204	16.5
Total	1236	100.0

Mean: 1.786 **Median:** 2.000

1. Variation for the public's attitude toward government spending to improve the conditions of African Americans is
   a. toward the low end.
   b. toward the high end.
   c. moderate.
   d. There is not enough information to answer the question.

2. The ___ is the appropriate measure of central tendency to use with the table.
   a. mode
   b. median
   c. mean
   d. The mode and mean are both appropriate for this table.
   e. Each measure is appropriate to use with the table.

3. The value of the appropriate measure of central tendency for the table is
   a. too little.
   b. just right.
   c. too much.
   d. 563.
   e. 2.00.

Use Table 7-7 to respond to Questions 4, 5, 6, and 7. The table depicts the public's attitude toward spending to improve the conditions of African Americans by their income level.

Table 7-7 Level of Income

Attitude	Low	Middle	High
Too little	48.1	40.5	27.0
Just right	41.3	43.5	51.4
Too much	10.6	16.0	21.6

Nominal Statistics:
Chi-square: 39.244 (Prob. = 0.000)
V: 0.130 C: 0.180
Lambda: 0.013 Lambda: 0.035 Lambda: 0.023

Ordinal Statistics:
Gamma: 0.252 Tau b: 0.162 Tau c: 0.156
Dyx: 0.157 Dxy: 0.167
Prob. = 0.000

4. Which income group is most supportive of the current level of spending to improve the conditions of African Americans?
   a. the low income group
   b. the middle income group
   c. the high income group
   d. There is no difference between the level of support among the three groups.
5. There are ___ degrees of freedom associated with the table.
   a. 1
   b. 2
   c. 4
   d. 6
6. The ___ statistic is the appropriate statistic to use with the table.
   a. Cramer's V
   b. Tau-b
   c. Tau-c
   d. Lambda
7. By knowing an individual's level of income you can reduce the prediction error associated with their attitude toward spending on improving the conditions of African Americans by ___ percent.
   a. 13
   b. 16.2
   c. 15.6
   d. 3.5

Table 7-8 Level of Confidence in the Military

Attitude	Great Deal	Only Some	Hardly Any
Too little	31.4	23.0	18.7
Just right	51.0	48.3	27.5
Too much	17.6	28.7	53.8

Nominal Statistics:
Chi-square: 51.839 (Prob. = 0.000)
V: 0.174 C: 0.239
Lambda: 0.023 Lambda: 0.053 Lambda: 0.039

Ordinal Statistics:
Gamma: 0.292 Tau b: 0.182 Tau c: 0.167
Dyx: 0.190 Dxy: 0.174
Prob. = 0.000

Use Table 7-8 to respond to Questions 8, 9, and 10. The table depicts the public's support for defense spending by public confidence in the military.

8. Which group is most supportive of the current level of defense spending?
   a. the group having a great deal of confidence in the military
   b. the group having only some confidence in the military
   c. the group having hardly any confidence in the military
   d. There is no difference between the level of support among the three groups.
9. The ___ statistic is the appropriate statistic to use with the table.
   a. Cramer's V
   b. Tau-b
   c. Tau-c
   d. Lambda
10. By knowing an individual's level of confidence in the military you can reduce the prediction error associated with their attitude toward defense spending by ___ percent.
   a. 17.4
   b. 18.2
   c. 16.7
   d. 5.3

Chapter 8

Comparative Politics

Outline

8-1 Introduction

Comparative politics is a broad and challenging subfield of study in political science. Comparative analyses require that the world's political systems be examined in a relative way. In addition, comparative scholars constantly debate the proper way to accomplish analyses. The subfield, however, allows political scientists to develop theories about politics and government to enhance the understanding of other nations.

There are two major approaches political scientists use when comparing governments. First, researchers will only compare similar political systems, such as the United States and the United Kingdom. When comparing nations with similar systems, the focus is on comparisons rather than contrasts. Or, researchers will concentrate on governments with dissimilar systems. When they concentrate on countries with dissimilar systems, such as the United States and Afghanistan, the concern starts with contrasts.

In this workbook chapter you will use each approach. You will examine dissimilar governments when analyzing differences in societal norms throughout the world. You will also use this approach when trying to learn why the people of some nations have greater pride in their nation than the people of other nations. You will examine similar governments when analyzing the political culture of American states. Before you start working on the exercises in this chapter, you should have a thorough understanding of Chapter 7 in the textbook.

8-2 Examining Societal Norms throughout the World

8-2a Exercise One

So far, you have found out that Americans have different ideas about the value pursuits of government. You have also identified reasons for the differences. Conservatives, for example, want the government to maintain order. Liberals, on the other hand, want the government to promote equality. Examine attitudes about several value issues in other nations of the world.

→ Data File: **NATIONS**
→ Task: **ANALYZE—DESCRIPTIVE STATISTICS—FREQUENCIES**
→ Variable 1: **ABUNWANT**
→ Variable 2: **KIDMANNE**
→ Variable 3: **RACISM**
→ Variable 4: **CHEATTAX**
→ Variable 5: **EXMARRY**
→ Variable 6: **EUTHANAS**
→ Variable 7: **SMOKEDOP**
→ View 1: **FREQUENCIES**
→ View 2: **STATISTICS—MEAN—MEDIAN—STD. DEVIATION**

After you are familiar with the SPSSW output, fill in Table 8-1 and respond to the questions that follow.

1. Which value issue has the greatest level of public support?

2. Which value issue has the lowest level of public support?

3. Which value issue has more high scores that affected the mean?

4. Which value issue has more low scores that affected the mean?

Table 8-1 Examining Societal Norms throughout the World

Variable	Median	Mean	Stand Dev.
ABUNWANT			
KIDMANNE			
RACISM			
CHEATTAX			
EXMARRY			
EUTHANAS			
SMOKEDOP			

5. Which value issue has more variation in its range of scores?

6. Which value issue has the least variation in its range of scores?

7. What is the appropriate measure of central tendency to use with the **ABUNWANT** variable? Circle one.

Median **Mean**

8. How do the results in the table compare with the attitudes that the American public has for these value issues?

9. Based on the results, briefly describe societal values throughout the world.

What socialization agents influence societal values throughout the nations of the world? To explore this question, examine the relationship between the extent of religious activity (**RELACTIV**)in a nation and societal values (**VALUES**). Before you try to determine whether there is a relationship, respond to the questions that follow. Then state a research and a null hypothesis for the relationship that you expect to find between the two variables.

Note: You will not use a sample in this exercise because the entire population of nations is available. Therefore, questions dealing with statistical significance will be skipped to concentrate on the strength of the relationship.

10. What is the level of measurement for the dependent variable? Circle one.

Nominal **Ordinal** **Interval** **Ratio**

11. What is the level of measurement for the independent variable? Circle one.

Nominal **Ordinal** **Interval** **Ratio**

12. What is the variable description for the **VALUES** variable?

13. Which variable is the dependent variable? Circle one.

VALUES **RELACTIV**

Research Hypothesis:

Null Hypothesis:

→ Data File: **NATIONS**
→ Task: **GRAPHS—SCATTER—SIMPLE**
→ Y Axis: **VALUES**
→ X Axis: **RELACTIV**

14. What is the direction of the relationship?

15. Succinctly describe the relationship.

→ Task: **ANALYZE—REGRESSION—LINEAR**
→ Dependent Variable: **VALUES**
→ Independent Variable: **RELACTIV**
→ View: **REGRESSION**

After you examine the SPSSW output, respond to the following questions.

16. How many nations are included in the analysis?

17. What is the value of the Pearson correlation coefficient (R)?

18. What is the value of the R-Square statistic?

19. According to the statistic, how much of the variation in a nation's societal values is accounted for by the extent of religious activity?

20. What is the value of the Y intercept?

21. What is the value of the unstandardized regression coefficient (slope)?

22. Use the results to depict the regression equation.

23. Succinctly describe the effect the independent variable has on societal values throughout the world.

You have seen that the extent of religious activity in a nation contributes to societal values. What other factors might help to explain more variation in societal values? In addition, to the extent of religious activity, examine the effects of newspaper circulation and the literacy rate.

→ Data File: **NATIONS**
→ Task: **ANALYZE—REGRESSION—LINEAR**
→ Dependent Variable: **VALUES**
→ Independent Variable 1: **RELACTIV**
→ Independent Variable 2: **PAPERS**
→ Independent Variable 3: **LITERACY**
→ View: **REGRESSION**

After you examine the SPSSW output, respond to the following questions.

Note: For this exercise, pretend that you are working with a sample. Thus, some of the questions deal with statistical significance.

24. What percentage of the variation in a nation's societal values is explained by the variables?

25. What is the unstandardized regression coefficient for each of the following variables?

RELACTIV ___________
PAPERS ___________
LITERACY ___________

26. What are the beta coefficients for each of the following variables?

RELACTIV ___________
PAPERS ___________
LITERACY ___________

27. Which of the independent variables has the greatest effect on a nation's societal values?

28. Which independent variable has the least effect?

29. Is each of the variables statistically significant?

Y **N**

30. Which variable(s) is/are not statistically significant?

Rerun the regression procedure without the variables that are not significant.

31. Which independent variable has the greatest effect in the new regression model?

32. What percentage of the variation in a nation's societal values is explained by the variables?

8-3 Examining National Pride

8-3a Exercise Two

Why do the people in some nations have more national pride than the citizens of other nations? Perhaps nations that have developed a national identity have more pride. You read in Chapter 7 of your text that a major hurdle during the development of a nation is the need for citizens to develop a national identity. Failure to achieve a national identity can lead to disassociation with one's country, cultural conflict, and even civil war. This crisis is particularly acute in third-world nations where tribal identity can take precedent over national goals.

The United States, however, has also experienced national identity problems. During the Civil War, for example, Southern pride was prevalent. And the 1960s saw the emergence of Black Pride and the need for groups to identify with their roots. Subsequently, government and educational institutions were pressed to recognize and offer courses dealing with the diverse cultures of Americans. These divergent demands caused resentment in America. Many members of the majority race were concerned that America was losing its national identity and becoming a "hyphenated" nation. Instead of simply identifying themselves as Americans, for example, many began to identify themselves as African Americans, Muslim Americans, or Mexican Americans. See if there is a relationship between the population heterogeneity of a nation (**MULTICUL**) and national pride (**NATLPRID**).

Before you try to determine whether there is a relationship, however, respond to the following questions. Then state a research and a null hypothesis for the relationship that you expect to find between the two variables.

33. What is the level of measurement for the dependent variable? Circle one.

Nominal **Ordinal** **Interval** **Ratio**

34. What is the level of measurement for the independent variable? Circle one.

Nominal **Ordinal** **Interval** **Ratio**

35. What is the variable description for the **NATLPRID** variable?

36. Which variable is the dependent variable? Circle one.

NATLPRID **MULTICUL**

Research Hypothesis:

Null Hypothesis:

→ Data File: **NATIONS**
→ Task: **GRAPHS—SCATTER—SIMPLE**
→ Y Axis: **NATLPRID**
→ X Axis: **MULTICUL**

37. What is the direction of the relationship?

38. Succinctly describe the relationship.

→ Task: **ANALYZE—REGRESSION—LINEAR**
→ Dependent Variable: **NATLPRID**
→ Independent Variable: **MULTICUL**
→ View: **REGRESSION**

After you examine the SPSSW output, respond to the following questions.

39. How many nations are included in the analysis?

40. What is the value of the Pearson correlation coefficient (R)?

41. What is the value of the R-Square statistic?

42. According to the statistic, how much of the variation in the national pride of a nation is accounted for by the diversity of the population?

43. What is the value of the Y intercept?

44. What is the value of the unstandardized regression coefficient (slope)?

45. Use the results to depict the regression equation.

46. Is this relationship statistically significant?

Y **N**

47. Do you reject the null hypothesis?

Y **N**

48. Succinctly describe the effect that population diversity has on national pride throughout the world.

You have seen that the extent of population diversity in a nation contributes to national pride. What other factors might help to explain more variation in national pride? In addition, to the extent of population diversity, examine the effects of religious activity, one's satisfaction with life, the literacy rate, and one's attitude toward societal values.

→ Data File: **NATIONS**
→ Task: **ANALYZE—REGRESSION—LINEAR**
→ Dependent Variable: **NATLPRID**
→ Independent Variable 1: **MULTICUL**
→ Independent Variable 2: **RELACTIV**
→ Independent Variable 3: **HAPPY**

→ Independent Variable 4: **LITERACY**
→ Independent Variable 5: **VALUES**
→ View: **REGRESSION**

After you examine the SPSSW output, respond to the following questions.

49. What percentage of the variation in a nation's national pride is explained by the variables?

50. What is the unstandardized regression coefficient for each variable?

MULTICUL ____________
RELACTIV ____________
HAPPY ____________
LITERACY ____________
VALUES ____________

51. What are the beta coefficients for each variable?

MULTICUL ____________
RELACTIV ____________
HAPPY ____________
LITERACY ____________
VALUES ____________

52. Which of the independent variables has the greatest effect on a nation's level of national pride?

53. Which independent variable has the least effect?

54. Is each of the variables statistically significant?

Y **N**

55. Which variable(s) is/are not statistically significant?

Rerun the regression procedure without the variables that are not significant.

56. Which independent variable has the greatest effect in the new regression model?

57. What percentage of the variation in a nation's level of national pride is explained by the variables?

8-4 Examining Political Culture in the United States

8-4a Exercise Three

In *American Federalism: A View from the States,* Daniel Elazar wrote that America's regions and states reflected a particular set of attitudes and general behavior patterns that shaped a state's politics and ultimately its policy formulation and adoption. He also identified three distinct political subcultures in the United States: traditionalistic, individualistic, and moralistic subcultures. Each subculture addressed three major questions. What is the proper role of government in society? What is the proper means of participation in society? How are the government institutions and officeholders performing their duties?

According to Elazar, in the *traditionalistic* political subculture, the community is dominated by a small, self-perpetuating, paternalistic ruling elite and large, compliant nonelite. There is a hierarchical arrangement to the political order that serves to limit the power and influence of the general public while allocating authority to a few individuals. Public policy reflects the interests of those who exercise influence and control. The benefits of public policy disproportionately go to the elite. Family and social relationships form the basis for maintaining the elite structure in lieu of mass participation. The major purpose of government is to maintain order. Thus, one would find a prevalence of regulatory policies in effect. In addition, the political system is closed and limited to elite participation. The roots of this subculture are in the pre-industrial, agrarian South.

An *individualistic* region or state, on the other hand, emphasizes the goals, aspirations, and initiative of private individuals or groups. Politics and government function as a marketplace and the government exists to provide those functions demanded by the people. In addition, government is reactive, limited and not intrusive in the lives of citizens. Politics is not a high calling but is like any other business venture. Thus, skill and talent prevail and the citizen can expect economic and social benefits. The goals of the government are to protect the interests of the business elite, provide public goods and services as demanded, and protect the economy from unnecessary government intrusion. This subculture's roots are in the mercantile centers of the Eastern seaboard.

A *moralistic* area is characterized by a public-spirited citizenry dedicated to the common betterment of all its members. Widespread political participation is valued and expected. The community's politicians are dedicated, selfless, and incorruptible leaders. Politics is a duty and a higher calling not to be used for personal gain and advantage. The primary goal is to promote the general welfare and insure a fair economic system achieved through positive government intervention. The roots of this subculture are in Puritan New England.

Look at the distribution of political culture in America.

→ Data File: **STATES**
→ Task: **ANALYZE—DESCRIPTIVE STATISTICS—FREQUENCIES**
→ Variable: **ELAZARPC**
→ View 1: **FREQUENCIES**
→ View 2: **STATISTICS—MEAN—MEDIAN—MODE**
→ View 3: **CHARTS—PIE CHARTS**

After you are familiar with the SPSSW output, respond to the following questions.

58. What is the level of measurement for this variable? Circle one.

Nominal **Ordinal** **Interval** **Ratio**

59. Which of the measures of central tendency is the most appropriate to use? Circle one.

Mode **Median** **Mean**

60. What is the value of the appropriate measure of central tendency?

61. How many states are included in the analysis?

62. Briefly discuss the distribution.

According to Elazar, regional political views were, in part, affected by the migration of religious groups. The moralistic subculture, for example, is characterized by concentrations of Mormons, Lutherans, Jews, and Quakers. One would find members of the Church of Christ, Methodists and Catholics in an individualistic region. In a traditionalistic subculture, on the other hand, one would find Baptists and members of the more conservative Protestant religions. Now examine religious concentrations in the states.

Note: You will not use a sample in this exercise because the entire population of U.S. states is available. Therefore, questions dealing with statistical significance will be skipped to concentrate on the strength of the relationship.

→ Data File: **STATES**
→ Task: **ANALYZE—DESCRIPTIVE STATISTICS—CROSSTABS**
→ Row Variable: **ELAZARPC**
→ Column Variable 1: **CNORELIG**
→ Column Variable 2: **CJEWISH**
→ Column Variable 3: **CCATHOLI**
→ Column Variable 4: **CBAPTIST**
→ View 1: **STATISTICS—PHI AND CRAMER'S V**
→ View 2: **CELLS—PERCENTAGE—COLUMN**

Table 8-2 Political Culture by Religious Affiliation

Subculture	CNORELIG		CJEWISH		CCATHOLI		CBAPTIST	
	Mode	%	*Mode*	%	*Mode*	%	*Mode*	%
Traditionalistic	L	50.0						
Individualistic								
Moralistic								
Cramer's V								

1. Mode = Modal category
2. L = Low
3. M = Moderate
4. H = High
5. % = Percent of states in the modal category

When you are familiar with the SPSSW output, fill in Table 8-2. Then use the output and the table to respond to the questions that follow.

63. Which religious group is least prevalent in the traditionalistic states? Circle one.

CNORELIG **CJEWISH** **CCATHOLI** **CBAPTIST**

64. Which religious group is most prevalent in the traditionalistic states? Circle one.

CNORELIG **CJEWISH** **CCATHOLI** **CBAPTIST**

65. Which religious group is least prevalent in the individualistic states? Circle one.

CNORELIG **CJEWISH** **CCATHOLI** **CBAPTIST**

66. Which religious group is most prevalent in the individualistic states? Circle one.

CNORELIG **CJEWISH** **CCATHOLI** **CBAPTIST**

67. Which religious group is least prevalent in the moralistic states? Circle one.

CNORELIG **CJEWISH** **CCATHOLI** **CBAPTIST**

68. Which religious group is most prevalent in the moralistic states? Circle one.

CNORELIG **CJEWISH** **CCATHOLI** **CBAPTIST**

69. Based on the results of your analyses, describe the relationship between the prevalence of religious groups and the political subculture of a state.

70. What do the results suggest about Elazar's writings concerning religious concentrations and the states?

The extent of political participation varies within the three political subcultures. In review, political participation in a traditionalistic subculture is limited to the political elite. Thus, it is at one end of a participation continuum. At one time, for example, poll taxes, annual voter registration, and other deterrents to participation existed. At the opposite end of the continuum is the moralistic subculture. The political system in a moralistic subculture is very open and encouraging of participation. North Dakota and Wisconsin, for example, do not require pre-registration for voting. The individualistic subculture falls between the other two subcultures on the continuum. Consequently, participation is neither discouraged (traditionalistic) nor encouraged (moralistic). Participation is strictly up to the individual. Examine the extent of political participation in the subcultures to see if there are differences.

→ Data File: **STATES**
→ Task: **ANALYZE—DESCRIPTIVE STATISTICS—CROSSTABS**
→ Row Variable 1: **CVOTED**
→ Row Variable 2: **CREGVOTE**
→ Row Variable 3: **CMOTORVO**
→ Column Variable: **ELAZARPC**
→ View 1: **STATISTICS—PHI AND CRAMER'S V**
→ View 2: **CELLS—PERCENTAGE—COLUMN**

When you are familiar with the SPSSW output, fill in Table 8-3. Then use the output and the table to respond to the questions that follow.

Table 8-3 Political Participation by Political Culture

Political Activity	Traditionalistic		Individualistic		Moralistic		Cramer's V	
	Mode	%	*Mode*	%	*Mode*	%	*Mode*	%
CVOTED	L	68.8						
CREGVOTE								
CMOTORVO								

1. Mode = Modal category
2. L = Low
3. M = Moderate
4. H = High
5. % = Percent of states in the modal category

71. Which form of political participation has the lowest level of participation in the traditionalistic states? Circle one.

CVOTED CREGVOTE CMOTORVO

72. Which form of political participation has the highest level of participation in the traditionalistic states? Circle one.

CVOTED CREGVOTE CMOTORVO

73. Which form of political participation has the lowest level of participation in the individualistic states? Circle one.

CVOTED CREGVOTE CMOTORVO

74. Which form of political participation has the highest level of participation in the individualistic states? Circle one.

CVOTED CREGVOTE CMOTORVO

75. Which form of political participation has the lowest level of participation in the moralistic states? Circle one.

CVOTED **CREGVOTE** **CMOTORVO**

76. Which form of political participation has the highest level of participation in the moralistic states? Circle one.

CVOTED **CREGVOTE** **CMOTORVO**

77. Based on the results of your analyses, describe the relationship between the extent of political participation and the political subculture of a state.

78. What do the results suggest about Elazar's writings concerning political participation and the states?

People have different views about the proper role of government in society in the three subcultures. In the traditionalistic subculture, the primary role of government is to maintain order. A major purpose of the government in a traditionalistic subculture is to provide public goods and services as demanded. And in the moralistic subculture, the main objective of government is to promote the general welfare. In this section you will examine three public policy areas to see if state spending differs between the subcultures. First, see if there are different levels of support for public education between the subcultures. Before you try to determine whether there is a relationship, state a research and a null hypothesis for the relationship that you expect to find between the two variables.

Research Hypothesis:

Null Hypothesis:

→ Data File: **STATES**
→ Task: **ANALYZE—DESCRIPTIVE STATISTICS—CROSSTABS**
→ Row Variable: **CEDUC$**
→ Column Variable: **ELAZARPC**
→ View 1: **STATISTICS—PHI AND CRAMER'S V**
→ View 2: **CELLS—PERCENTAGE—COLUMN**

After you examine the SPSSW output, respond to the following questions.

79. What primary purpose of government does the **CEDUC$** variable measure? Circle one.

Maintain Order **Provide Public Goods/Services** **Promote Equality**

80. Compare the percentages horizontally and describe the pattern.

81. What is the value of the Cramer's V statistic for this relationship?

82. Even though you have the entire population, what might explain the level of significance for this relationship?

83. Based on the results of your analyses, describe the relationship between the extent of state support for public education and the political subculture of a state.

Now see if there are different levels of support for prison funding in the subcultures. Before you try to determine whether there is a relationship, state a research and a null hypothesis for the relationship that you expect to find between the two variables.

Research Hypothesis:

Null Hypothesis:

→ Data File: **STATES**
→ Task: **ANALYZE—DESCRIPTIVE STATISTICS—CROSSTABS**
→ Row Variable: **CJAIL$**
→ Column Variable: **ELAZARPC**
→ View 1: **STATISTICS—PHI AND CRAMER'S V**
→ View 2: **CELLS—PERCENTAGE—COLUMN**

After you examine the SPSSW output, respond to the following questions.

84. What primary purpose of government does the **CJAIL$** variable measure? Circle one.

Maintain Order **Provide Public Goods/Services** **Promote Equality**

85. Compare the percentages horizontally and describe the pattern.

86. What is the value of the Cramer's V statistic for this relationship?

87. Even though the example analyzes the entire population, what might explain the level of significance for this relationship?

88. Based on the results of your analyses, describe the relationship between the extent of state support for prisons and the political subculture of a state.

Now see if there are different levels of support for welfare funding between the subcultures. Before you try to determine whether there is a relationship, state a research and a null hypothesis for the relationship that you expect to find between the two variables.

Research Hypothesis:

Null Hypothesis:

→ Data File:	**STATES**
→ Task:	**ANALYZE—DESCRIPTIVE STATISTICS—CROSSTABS**
→ Row Variable:	**CWELF$**
→ Column Variable:	**ELAZARPC**
→ View 1:	**STATISTICS—PHI AND CRAMER'S V**
→ View 2:	**CELLS—PERCENTAGE—COLUMN**

After you examine the SPSSW output, respond to the following questions.

89. What primary purpose of government does the **CWELF$** variable measure? Circle one.

Maintain Order **Provide Public Goods/Services** **Promote Equality**

90. Compare the percentages horizontally and describe the pattern.

91. What is the value of the Cramer's V statistic for this relationship?

92. Even though you have the entire population, what might explain the level of significance for this relationship?

93. Based on the results of your analyses, describe the relationship between the extent of state support for welfare funding and the political subculture of a state.

Now see whom the voters in the subcultures supported in the 2000 presidential campaign. Before you run the SPSSW Guide, however, respond to the following questions.

94. Which political subculture do you think will be most supportive of Vice President Al Gore? Circle one.

Traditionalistic **Individualistic** **Moralistic**

95. Which political subculture do you think will be least supportive of Vice President Al Gore? Circle one.

Traditionalistic **Individualistic** **Moralistic**

96. Which political subculture do you think will be most supportive of George Bush? Circle one.

Traditionalistic **Individualistic** **Moralistic**

97. Which political subculture do you think will be least supportive of George Bush? Circle one.

Traditionalistic **Individualistic** **Moralistic**

98. Which political subculture do you think will be most supportive of Ralph Nader? Circle one.

Traditionalistic **Individualistic** **Moralistic**

99. Which political subculture do you think will be least supportive of Ralph Nader? Circle one.

Traditionalistic Individualistic Moralistic

→ Data File: **STATES**
→ Task: **ANALYZE—DESCRIPTIVE STATISTICS—CROSSTABS**
→ Row Variable 1: **CBUSH**
→ Row Variable 2: **CGORE**
→ Row Variable 3: **CNADER**
→ Column Variable: **ELAZARPC**
→ View 1: **STATISTICS—PHI AND CRAMER'S V**
→ View 2: **CELLS—PERCENTAGE—COLUMN**

When you are familiar with the SPSSW output, fill in Table 8-4. Then use the output and the table to respond to the questions that follow.

Table 8-4 Presidential Vote by Political Culture (%)

	Traditionalistic		Individualistic		Moralistic		
Candidate	*Low*	*High*	*Low*	*High*	*Low*	*High*	*Cramer's V*
Bush							
Gore							
Nader							

100. Do the results support the predictions you made in Questions 94–99?

Y N

101. Interpret the Cramer's V statistics for each of the relationships.

102. Based on the results of your analyses, describe the relationship between presidential voting and the political subculture of a state.

103. What do the results suggest about Elazar's writings concerning presidential voting and the states?

Chapter Quiz

Chapter Quiz

1. When political scientists concentrate on countries with dissimilar systems, such as the United States and Afghanistan, the primary research concern starts with
   a. comparisons.
   b. contrasts.
   c. similarities.
   d. The primary research concern involves a and b.

2. When political scientists study nations with similar systems, such as the United States and Great Britain, the primary research focus is on
   a. comparisons.
   b. contrasts.
   c. disparities.
   d. The primary research concern involves a and b.

Use the pie chart in Figure 8-1 to respond to Questions 3 and 4. The chart depicts the national level of support citizens throughout the world have for homosexuality.

3. The level of variation for the variable is
   a. toward the low end.
   b. moderate.
   c. toward the high end.
   d. There is no difference in the categories of support.

4. What is the modal response?
   a. high
   b. moderate
   c. low
   d. It is a bimodal distribution.

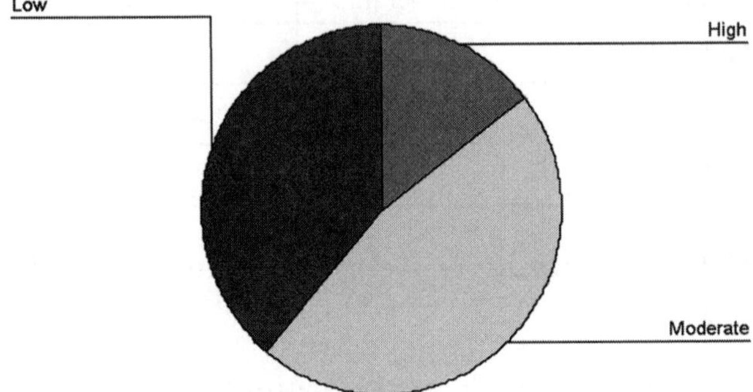

Figure 8-1
Percent Who Believe Homosexuality Is Never Acceptable Behavior

Use Table 8-5 to respond to Questions 5, 6, and 7. The table depicts the extent of pride citizens of the world have in their nation and the extent of diversity in the population of their nation.

Table 8-5 Extent of Population Diversity

Extent of Pride	Low	Moderate	High
Low	34.1	27.3	16.7
Moderate	47.8	18.2	16.7
High	17.4	54.5	66.6

5. Based on the results there is ___ relationship between the two variables.
   a. a weak
   b. a moderate
   c. a strong
   d. no
6. What is the direction of the relationship?
   a. positive
   b. negative
   c. curvilinear
   d. There is no relationship.
7. The ___ statistic is the appropriate measure of association to use with the table.
   a. Cramer's V
   b. Lambda
   c. Tau-b
   d. Tau-c

Use the pie chart in Figure 8-2 to respond to Questions 8 and 9.

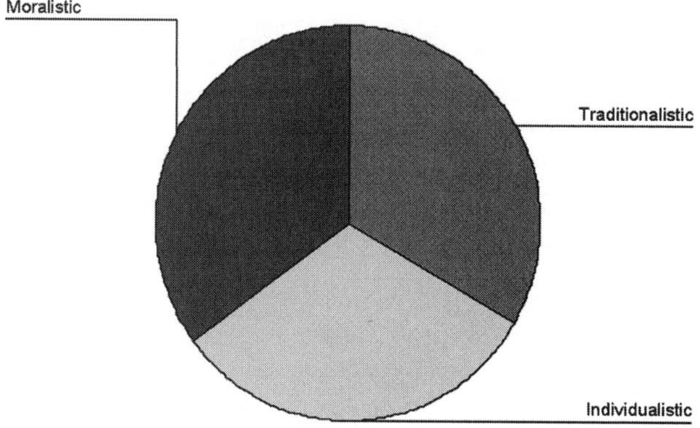

Figure 8-2
Political Culture in the United States

8. The level of variation for the variable is
   a. toward the low end.
   b. moderate.
   c. toward the high end.
   d. There is no difference in the categories of support.
9. What is the modal response?
   a. traditionalistic
   b. individualistic
   c. moralistic
   d. There appears to be more than one modal response.
10. Based on the workbook exercises, residents of the moralistic political subculture were more supportive of ___ in the 2000 presidential elections.
   a. Al Gore
   b. George W. Bush
   c. Ralph Nader
   d. Their support was equally distributed between Al Gore and Ralph Nader.

Chapter 9

International Relations

Outline

9-1 Introduction

Chapter 8 of your textbook considers relationships between nations. One point the chapter demonstrates is that international politics, like all politics, is a struggle for power. In today's apprehensive world, nations try to reduce their uncertainty by expanding their capacity to use political resources to influence the actions of other nations.

The chapter also looks at the causes of warfare, which is one of the most intriguing questions posed by scholars of international relations. War and conflict are as old as man's history. Today, however, the existence of weapons of mass destruction makes the question even more compelling because many nations now have the means to destroy each other and themselves.

This workbook chapter will examine the struggle for power, available political resources that enhance a nation's power (power sources), and reasons why some nations go to war more often than other nations. Before you start working on the exercises in this chapter, you should have a thorough understanding of Chapter 8 in the textbook.

9-2 Examining an Economic Dimension of Power

9-2a Exercise One

World leaders want to insure the continued existence of their people. This requires that they act to amplify the political resources that increase their nation's power and stature in the international system. Political scientists have grouped these resources into three broad categories: economic, military and psychological.

The most obvious way that economics affects international politics is through the relationship between wealth and military power. However, economics also affects international power in other ways. Today's world, for example, is economically interdependent. Trade is an important part of most domestic economies. Recall that during the 1970s the Organization of Petroleum Exporting Countries (OPEC) blocked the sale of oil to the Western world. Consequently oil prices soared, there were long lines at the gas pumps, and industrialized nations experienced economic downturns. America even nationalized speed limits at 55 mph to help conserve fuel. Industrialized nations can also influence the activities of poor nations by providing and threatening to withhold aid. Even the relationships between rich nations have a strong economic element. American industries, for example, are very dependent on Japanese computer chips. Additionally, the United States has a large trade deficit with Japan. As a result, Japan has become very important to the American economy and politics.

Examine several variables that measure the economic dimension of nations.

→ Data File: **NATIONS**
→ Task: **ANALYZE—DESCRIPTIVE STATISTICS—FREQUENCIES**
→ Variable 1: **GDP**
→ Variable 2: **TRADE**
→ Variable 3: **EXTDEBT**
→ View 1: **FREQUENCIES**
→ View 2: **STATISTICS—MEAN—MEDIAN—MODE—STD. DEVIATION MINIMUM—MAXIMUM**

Here the **GDP** variable measures a nation's gross domestic product in billions of American dollars for 1997. The **TRADE** variable measures a nation's total imports and exports in millions of American dollars for 1995. The **EXTDEBT** variable measures a nation's external debt in billions of American dollars for 1997.

After you are familiar with the SPSSW printout, answer the following questions.

1. What is the range of gross domestic product (GDP) for the lowest ten nations in 1997?

2. What is the range of gross domestic product (GDP) for the highest ten nations in 1997?

3. What percentage of nations had a GDP between $.33 billion and $5.90 billion dollars in 1997?

4. What was the mean value of GDP for the nations in 1997?

5. What was the median value of GDP for the nations in 1997?

6. Which of the measures of central tendency is the most appropriate to use? Circle one.

   Mode **Median** **Mean**

7. What were the minimum and maximum values of GDP for the nations in 1997?

   Minimum ____________
   Maximum ____________

8. What is the value of the standard deviation for the GDP for the nations in 1997?

9. Succinctly interpret the standard deviation for the GDP.

10. What is the range of total trade for the lowest ten nations in 1995?

11. What is the range of total trade for the highest ten nations in 1995?

12. What was the mean value of total trade for the nations in 1995?

13. What was the median value of total trade for the nations in 1995?

14. Which of the measures of central tendency is the most appropriate to use? Circle one.

Mode **Median** **Mean**

15. What were the minimum and maximum values of total trade for the nations in 1995?

Minimum ___________
Maximum ___________

16. What is the value of the standard deviation for total trade for the nations in 1995?

17. Succinctly interpret the standard deviation for the GDP.

18. What is the range of external debt for the lowest ten nations in 1997?

19. What is the range of external debt for the lowest ten nations in 1997?

20. What percentage of nations had an external debt rate between $.5 billion and $1.67 billion dollars in 1997?

21. What was the mean value of external debt for the nations in 1997?

22. What was the median value of external debt for the nations in 1997?

23. Which of the measures of central tendency is the most appropriate to use? Circle one.

Mode **Median** **Mean**

24. What were the minimum and maximum values of external debt for the nations in 1997?

Minimum ___________
Maximum ___________

25. What is the value of the standard deviation for the external debt for the nations in 1997?

26. Succinctly interpret the standard deviation for the external debt.

Now, look at the level of economic development for nations of the world.

→ Data File: **NATIONS**
→ Task: **ANALYZE—DESCRIPTIVE STATISTICS—FREQUENCIES**
→ Variable 1: **ECONDEVE**
→ View 1: **FREQUENCIES**
→ View 2: **STATISTICS—MEAN—MEDIAN—MODE**

Here the **ECONDEVE** variable measures the level of economic development for a nation.

After you are familiar with the SPSSW printout, answer the following questions.

27. How many nations are in the Least Developed category?

28. What is the percentage of the nations that are considered industrialized?

29. Which of the measures of central tendency is the most appropriate to use? Circle one.

Mode **Median** **Mean**

30. What is the value of the appropriate measure of central tendency?

9-3 Examining a Military Dimension of Power

9-3a Exercise Two

Today, the threat of violence or its actual use is the main way that nations try to impose their will on other nations. Consequently, a nation's military is a major power resource. As discussed in your textbook, military power is related to a nation's economic capacity. Industrialized nations have the potential for more military power than economically disadvantaged nations. While the amount and quality of a nation's economic capacity does not insure victory on the battlefield, a nation's military is an important part of a nation's prestige. Other nations may be deterred by one nation's willingness to use force if necessary to achieve the nation's goals.

Examine several variables that measure the military dimension of nations.

→ Data File: **NATIONS**
→ Task: **ANALYZE—DESCRIPTIVE STATISTICS—FREQUENCIES**
→ Variable 1: **INDUSTRY**
→ Variable 2: **DEFENSE$**

→ Variable 3: **MILITARY**
→ View 1: **FREQUENCIES**
→ View 2: **STATISTICS—MEAN—MEDIAN—MODE—STD. DEVIATION MINIMUM—MAXIMUM**

Here the **INDUSTRY** variable measures a nation's percent of the GDP accounted for by industry for 1997. The **DEFENSE$** variable measures a nation's percent of total expenditures allocated to defense in 1997. The **MILITARY** variable measures the size of a nation's military, in 1000s, for 1996.

After you are familiar with the SPSSW printout, answer the following questions.

31. What is the range of GDP accounted for by industry for the lowest ten nations in 1997?

32. What is the range of GDP accounted for by industry for the highest ten nations in 1997?

33. What was the mean value of GDP accounted for by industry for the nations in 1997?

34. What was the median value of GDP accounted for by industry for the nations in 1997?

35. Which of the measures of central tendency is the most appropriate to use? Circle one.

Mode **Median** **Mean**

36. What were the minimum and maximum values of GDP accounted for by industry for the nations in 1997?

Minimum ___________
Maximum ___________

37. What is the value of the standard deviation for the GDP accounted for by industry for the nations in 1997?

38. Succinctly interpret the standard deviation for the GDP accounted for by industry for the nations in 1997.

39. What is the range of a nation's percent of total expenditures allocated to defense for the lowest ten nations in 1997?

40. What is the range of a nation's percent of total expenditures allocated to defense for the highest ten nations in 1997?

41. What was the mean value of a nation's percent of total expenditures allocated to defense in 1997?

42. What was the mean value of a nation's percent of total expenditures allocated to defense in 1997?

43. Which of the measures of central tendency is the most appropriate to use? Circle one.

Mode **Median** **Mean**

44. What were the minimum and maximum values of a nation's percent of total expenditures allocated to defense in 1997?

Minimum ___________

Maximum ___________

45. What is the value of the standard deviation for a nation's percent of total expenditures allocated to defense in 1997?

46. Succinctly interpret the standard deviation for a nation's percent of total expenditures allocated to defense in 1997.

47. What is the range of the size of a nation's military for the lowest 15 nations in 1996?

48. What is the range of the size of a nation's military for the highest ten nations in 1996?

49. What was the mean value of the size of a nation's military in 1996?

50. What was the median value of the size of a nation's military in 1996?

51. Which of the measures of central tendency is the most appropriate to use? Circle one.

Mode **Median** **Mean**

52. What were the minimum and maximum values of the size of a nation's military in 1996?

Minimum ___________
Maximum ___________

53. What is the value of the standard deviation for the size of a nation's military in 1996?

54. Succinctly interpret the standard deviation for the size of a nation's military in 1996.

9-4 Examining a Psychological Dimension of Power

9-4a Exercise Three

Though intangible, a nation's psychological assets are also important sources of power. Political will, national morale, character, and leadership can influence political outcomes. Despite superior economic and military resources, for example, the United States and the Soviet Union could not impose their will on the people of Vietnam and Afghanistan. Superior firepower could not save the Shah of Iran from the fundamentalist ideas of the Ayatollah Khomeini. Likewise, the British were driven from India by the power of nationalism fueled by the ideas and commitment of Gandhi. These psychological resources are often manifested in the national pride of a nation.

Examine several variables that measure the psychological dimension of nations.

→ Data File: **NATIONS**
→ Task: **ANALYZE—DESCRIPTIVE STATISTICS—FREQUENCIES**
→ Variable 1: **NATLPRID**
→ Variable 2: **MULTICUL**
→ View 1: **FREQUENCIES**
→ View 2: **STATISTICS—MEAN—MEDIAN—MODE—STD. DEVIATION MINIMUM—MAXIMUM**

Here the **NATLPRID** variable measures the percent who say they are proud to be a citizen of their country. The **MULTICUL** variable measures the odds that any two persons will differ in their race, religion, ethnicity (tribe) or language group.

When you are familiar with the SPSSW output, answer the following questions.

55. What is the range of the percent who say they are proud to be a citizen of their country for the lowest ten nations?

56. What is the range of the percent who say they are proud to be a citizen of their country for the highest ten nations?

57. What was the mean value of the percent who say they are proud to be a citizen of their country?

58. What was the median value of the percent who say they are proud to be a citizen of their country?

59. Which of the measures of central tendency is the most appropriate to use? Circle one.

Mode **Median** **Mean**

60. What were the minimum and maximum values of the percent who say they are proud to be a citizen of their country?

Minimum ___________
Maximum ___________

61. What is the value of the standard deviation for the percent who say they are proud to be a citizen of their country?

62. Succinctly interpret the standard deviation for the percent who say they are proud to be a citizen of their country.

63. What is the range of the extent of multiculturalism for the lowest 30 nations?

64. What is the range of the extent of multiculturalism for the highest ten nations?

65. What was the mean value of the extent of multiculturalism?

66. What was the median value of the extent of multiculturalism?

67. Which of the measures of central tendency is the most appropriate to use? Circle one.

Mode **Median** **Mean**

68. What were the minimum and maximum values of the extent of multiculturalism?

Minimum __________
Maximum __________

69. What is the value of the standard deviation for the extent of multiculturalism?

70. Succinctly interpret the standard deviation for the extent of multiculturalism.

9-5 Examining the Causes of War

9-5a Exercise Four

Identifying the causes of war is an intriguing area of study for scholars of international relations. War and conflict have always characterized societies. Today, however, the global proliferation of weapons of mass destruction makes the issue even more critical. War is not just another way that nations try to achieve their goals. In today's world, terrorist groups such as Hamas also engage in armed conflicts to achieve independence. Consequently, the multiplicity of acts of international violence makes war and its causes a subject of deep interest.

This exercise will examine the effect that several factors have on the inclination for a nation to go to war. The factors to be examined are the power sources analyzed in the above exercises, forms of government and the character of a nation. First, however, examine the propensity for a nation to go to war.

→ Data File: **NATIONS**
→ Task: **ANALYZE—DESCRIPTIVE STATISTICS—FREQUENCIES**
→ Variable 1: **WAR**
→ View 1: **FREQUENCIES**
→ View 2: **STATISTICS—MEAN—MEDIAN—MODE**

Here the **WAR** variable measures the type of armed conflict nations were involved in from 1990 to 1996.

When you are familiar with the SPSSW output, answer the following questions.

71. How many nations have not been involved in some type of armed conflict from 1990 to 1996?

72. What percentage of the nations are/were involved in some type of armed conflict from 1990 to 1996?

73. What does the percentage suggest about the extent of armed conflict throughout the world?

74. Which of the measures of central tendency is the most appropriate to use? Circle one.

Mode **Median** **Mean**

75. What is the value of the appropriate measure of central tendency?

Now examine the effect that economic, military, and psychological variables have on a nation's involvement in wars.

→ Data File: **NATIONS**
→ Task: **ANALYZE—DESCRIPTIVE STATISTICS—CROSSTABS**
→ Row Variable: **WAR**
→ Column Variable 1: **ECONDEVE**
→ Column Variable 2: **CEXTDEBT**
→ Column Variable 3: **CDEFENSE**
→ Column Variable 4: **CMILITAR**
→ Column Variable 5: **CMULTICU**
→ Column Variable 6: **CNATPRID**
→ View 1: **STATISTICS—TAU B**
→ View 2: **CELLS—PERCENTAGE—COLUMN**

When you are familiar with the SPSSW output, fill in Table 9-1 that follows. Then use the output and the table to respond to the questions for this exercise.

Table **9-1 Type of Conflict by Power Source**

Conflict	ECONDEV		CEXTDEBT		CDEFENSE		CMILITAR		CMULTICUL		CNATPRID	
	Mode	%	*Mode*	%	*Mode*	%	*Mode*	%	*Mode*	%	*Mode*	%
None												
Civil War												
Interstate												
Tau b												
Significance												

1. Mode = Modal category
2. L = Low
3. M = Moderate
4. H = High
5. % = Percent of nations in the modal category

76. State a research hypothesis for the expected relationship between a nation's level of economic development and a nation's potential to go to war.

77. State a research hypothesis for the expected relationship between the size of a nation's level military and a nation's potential to go to war.

78. State a research hypothesis for the expected relationship between the level of national pride in a nation and a nation's potential to go to war.

79. Which variable has the strongest effect on a nation's potential to go to war? Circle one.

ECONDEVE	CEXTDEBT	CDEFENSE
CMILITAR	CMULTICU	CNATPRID

80. Which variable has the weakest effect on a nation's potential to go to war? Circle one.

ECONDEVE	CEXTDEBT	CDEFENSE
CMILITAR	CMULTICU	CNATPRID

81. Are all of the relationships statistically significant?

Y N

82. If you answered *no* to Question 81, which relationships are not statistically significant?

83. What do the results suggest about the causes of war?

Chapter Quiz

Use the histogram in Figure 9-1 to respond to Questions 1, 2, and 3. The histogram depicts the annual unemployment rate in nations of the world.

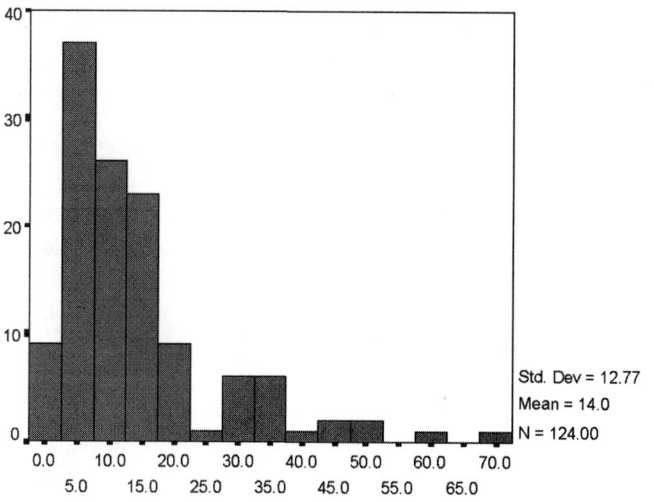

Figure 9-1
Annual Unemployment Rate in Nations of the World

1. The level of data for the variable is
   a. nominal.
   b. ordinal.
   c. interval.
   d. ratio.
2. The ___ is the appropriate measure of central tendency to use with the histogram.
   a. mode
   b. median
   c. mean
   d. It is appropriate to use each of the above measures with the histogram.
3. Approximately ___ nations have an annual unemployment rate greater than 40 percent.
   a. 1
   b. 6
   c. 15
   d. 20

Use the following SPSSW Guide to respond to Questions 4 and 5.

→ Data File:	**NATIONS**
→ Task:	**ANALYZE—DESCRIPTIVESTATISTICS—CROSSTABS**
→ Row Variable:	**WAR**
→ Column Variable 1:	**ECONDEVE**
→ Column Variable 2:	**CEXTDEBT**
→ View 1:	**STATISTICS—PHI AND CRAMER'S V**
→ View 2:	**CELLS—PERCENTAGE—COLUMN**

4. Which variable is the independent variable for this SPSSW Guide?
   a. **WAR**
   b. **ECONDEVE**
   c. **CEXTDEBT**
   d. Both b and c are independent variables.
5. How many cross-tabulation tables will be produced when you perform the SPSSW Guide?
   a. 1
   b. 2
   c. 3
   d. A table will be produced for each category of the independent variable(s).

Use Table 9-2 to respond to Questions 6 and 7. The table depicts statistics dealing with the relationship of a nation being involved in a war and a nation's level of external debt, the size of its military, extent of individual freedom, and the extent of national pride.

Table 9-2 Effect of Power Sources for a Nation Involved in War

Variable	Cramer's V	Significance
External debt	.12	.122
Military size	.20	.014
Extent of individual freedom	.24	.004
Extent of national pride	.37	.027

6. Which variable does not have a real relationship with a nation's propensity to go to war?
   a. external debt
   b. military size
   c. extent of individual freedom
   d. extent of national pride
7. Which variable has the strongest relationship with a nation's propensity to go to war?
   a. external debt
   b. military size
   c. extent of individual freedom
   d. extent of national pride

Use Table 9-3 to respond to Questions 8, 9, and 10. The table depicts the relationship between the size of a nation's military and the nation's Gross Domestic Product (GDP).

Table 9-3 Size of Military by Size of Gross Domestic Product (%)

	Size of Gross Domestic Product (%)		
Size of Military	*Low*	*Moderate*	*High*
Small	76.7	29.4	3.5
Moderate	18.6	52.9	28.1
Large	4.7	17.6	68.4

Measures of Association
Phi: .75
Cramer's V: .53
Lambda: .48
Tau b: .63

8. The table shows that there is a ___ relationship between the size of a nation's military and the nation's Gross Domestic Product.
   a. weak positive
   b. weak negative
   c. moderate positive
   d. strong negative
   e. strong positive
9. The ___ statistic is the appropriate measure of association to use with the table.
   a. Phi
   b. Cramer's V
   c. Lambda
   d. Tau-b
10. How much can a prediction of the size of a nation's military be improved by knowing the size of a nation's gross domestic product?
   a. 75 percent
   b. 53 percent
   c. 48 percent
   d. 63 percent

Chapter

Chapter 10

Data Entry

Outline

10-1 Introduction

In this chapter you will learn how to create and save SPSSW data files. As such, the chapter covers the following steps:

- Coding data
- Creating a new data file
- Entering data
- Saving the data file

Before you start working with this chapter, you should have a thorough understanding of Chapter 12 in the textbook.

10-2 Coding the Data

Coding is the process of assigning numbers to all possible responses to all questions or items that make up your database. Coding is necessary when working with nominal or ordinal data. With metric data, you do not have to assign numbers. Following is a review of the coding rules that you must follow when working with nominal and ordinal data.

1. Code numbers should make intuitive sense for variables that can be rank ordered. For example, higher scores should be assigned higher code numbers (1 = Low; 2 = Medium; 3 = High).
2. The coding categories must be mutually exclusive. That is, each unit of analysis should fit into one and only one category.
3. The coding scheme must be exhaustive. That is, every response must fit into a category with few responses being classified as "other."
4. Categories must be specific enough to capture differences while using the smallest possible number of categories.

Table 10-1 presents data that was collected for the ten largest cities in America. As you can see, all of the variables except for the name of the city are metric level data. Thus, you will not need to code these variables.

10-3 Creating a New Data File

The SPSSW Data Editor window provides a convenient spreadsheet method for creating and editing data files. The Data Editor window opens automatically when you start an SPSSW session. There are two views you can access in the window: a Data View and a Variable View. Simply click on one of the tabs in the lower left-hand corner of the window to access the desired view.

Before entering data into a new data file, you must define the attributes of the variables you will be working with. Thus, the first step is to display the Variable View (Figure 10-1). The column headings in the Variable View display definition information for the variables in a data set. For example, you can name variables (*Name*) and define attributes such as variable labels (*Label*), category value labels (*Values*), data type (*Type*), and user-defined missing values (*Missing*). Note that the rows beneath the column headings are blank.

Define the variable attributes for the City data set depicted in Table 10-1. Use the Variable View tab in the Data Editor window for this purpose (Figure 10-1).

The first step when defining variables is to type the name of the first variable (for example, **CITY**) in the column labeled *Name*. (Note: variable names must begin with a letter. The remaining characters can be any letter, any digit, a period, or the symbols @, #,_, or $. Variable names cannot end with a period or exceed

Table 10-1 Data for Selected Variables for Ten Largest U.S. Cities

CITY	CPOP	WPOP	BPOP	HPOP	AGE	POOR	CRIME	DROP
New York	7322.6	52.33	28.78	23.73	33.7	18.91	451246	50.71
Chicago	2783.7	45.48	39.03	19.23	31.3	21.28	209098	55.90
Los Angeles	3485.4	52.94	13.94	39.32	30.7	18.47	234207	57.81
Philadelphia	1585.6	53.54	39.89	5.31	33.2	19.76	80365	51.83
Houston	1630.9	52.76	28.06	27.16	30.4	20.42	117659	52.92
Detroit	1028.0	21.59	75.73	2.64	30.8	31.95	95190	62.69
Dallas	1007.6	55.42	29.50	20.33	30.6	17.66	93947	51.21
San Diego	1110.6	67.21	9.33	20.14	30.5	12.82	72009	49.94
Phoenix	983.4	81.73	5.21	19.74	31.1	13.97	84874	54.54
Baltimore	736.0	39.12	59.19	0.95	32.6	21.23	70520	57.05

Variable descriptions:
CITY: Name of city
CPOP: Central city population
WPOP: White population (%)
BPOP: Black population (%)
HPOP: Hispanic population (%)
AGE: Median age of the population
POOR: Percent of the population below the poverty line
CRIME: Number of property crimes
DROP: Percent of the population without a high-school diploma

eight characters. In addition, spaces and special characters (!, ?, and *) cannot be used). Thus, the variable name **V1** is acceptable, while the variable name **1V** is not. The variable name **TEST_5** would be acceptable, while the variable name **Test 5** would not.

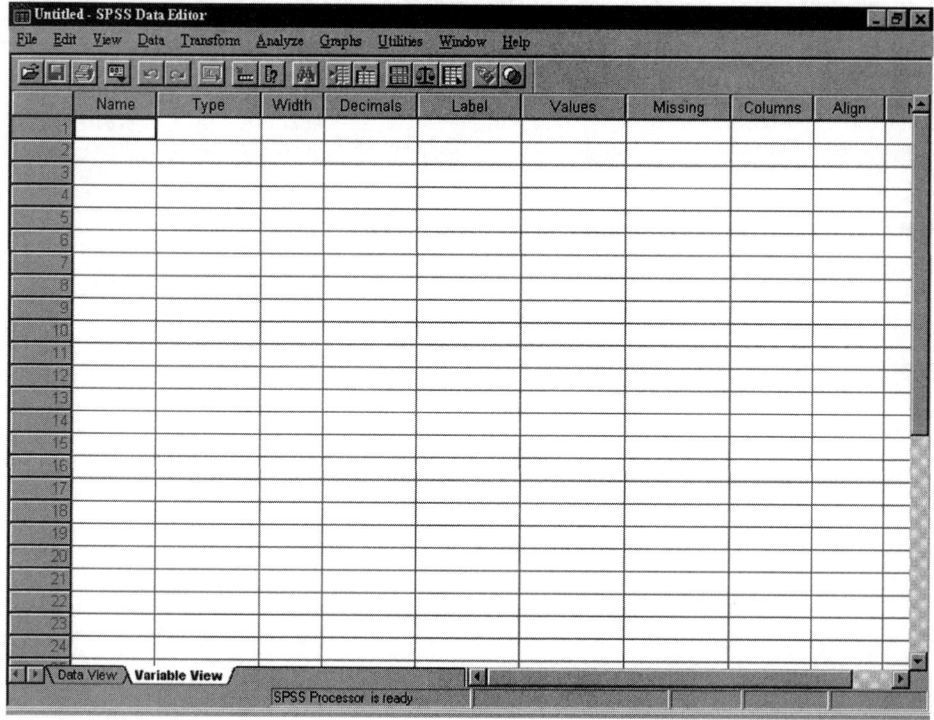

Figure 10-1
Data Editor Window, Variable View

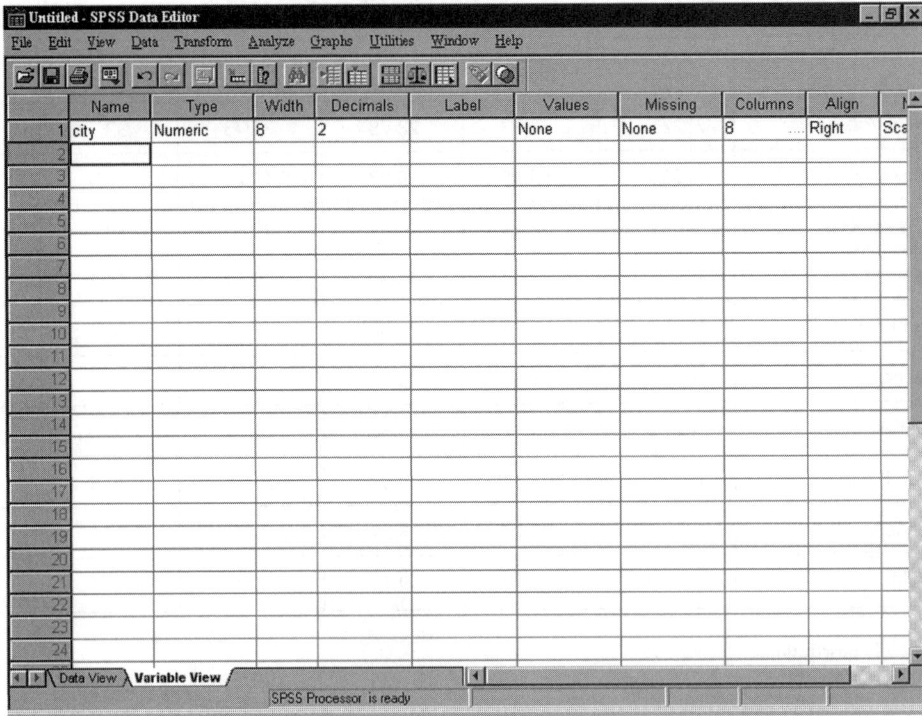

Figure 10-2
Data Editor Window, Variable View, Depicting Variable Definition

Move to the second row to enter the name of the second variable in the *Name* column. When you do this, SPSSW automatically defines several attributes for the **CITY** variable, such as *Type, Width,* and *Decimals* (Figure 10-2). You can edit these attributes after you have entered the names of each variable in the set. Now, enter the names of the remaining variables. When you are finished, the Data Editor window should resemble the one depicted in Figure 10-3.

Now label the variables. To do this simply move to the *Label* column and enter the labels for each variable from Table 10-1. "Name of city" and "Central city pop-

Figure 10-3
Data Editor Window, Variable View, Depicting City Data

Untitled - SPSS Data Editor

File Edit View Data Transform Analyze Graphs Utilities Window Help

	Name	Type	Width	Decimals	Label	Values	Missing	Columns	Align	M
1	city	Numeric	8	2		None	None	8	Right	Sca
2	cpop	Numeric	8	2		None	None	8	Right	Sca
3	wpop	Numeric	8	2		None	None	8	Right	Sca
4	bpop	Numeric	8	2		None	None	8	Right	Sca
5	hpop	Numeric	8	2		None	None	8	Right	Sca
6	age	Numeric	8	2		None	None	8	Right	Sca
7	poor	Numeric	8	2		None	None	8	Right	Sca
8	crime	Numeric	8	2		None	None	8	Right	Sca
9	drop	Numeric	8	2		None	None	8	Right	Sca

Data View Variable View

SPSS Processor is ready

Untitled - SPSS Data Editor

	Name	Type	Width	Decimals	Label	Values
1	city	Numeric	8	2	Name of city	None
2	cpop	Numeric	8	2	Central city population	None
3	wpop	Numeric	8	2	White population (%)	None
4	bpop	Numeric	8	2	Black population (%)	None
5	hpop	Numeric	8	2	Hispanic population (%)	None
6	age	Numeric	8	2	Median age of the population	None
7	poor	Numeric	8	2	Percent of the population below the poverty line	None
8	crime	Numeric	8	2	Number of property crimes	None
9	drop	Numeric	8	2	Percent of the population without a high school diploma	None

Data View / Variable View — SPSS Processor is ready

Figure 10-4
Data Editor Window, Variable View, Depicting City Data Variables with Labels

ulation," for example, are the labels for the first two variables. When you are finished, the Data Editor window (Variable View) should resemble the one depicted in Figure 10-4.

Before entering the actual data, you must edit the attributes in the Variable View. Each variable except for the **CITY** variable, is a numeric variable. **CITY** is a string variable. Thus, you need to change the variable type from numeric to string. Click on the cell under the *Type* column for **CITY.** Then, select the data type ("string") in the *Variable Type* dialog box (Figure 10-5).

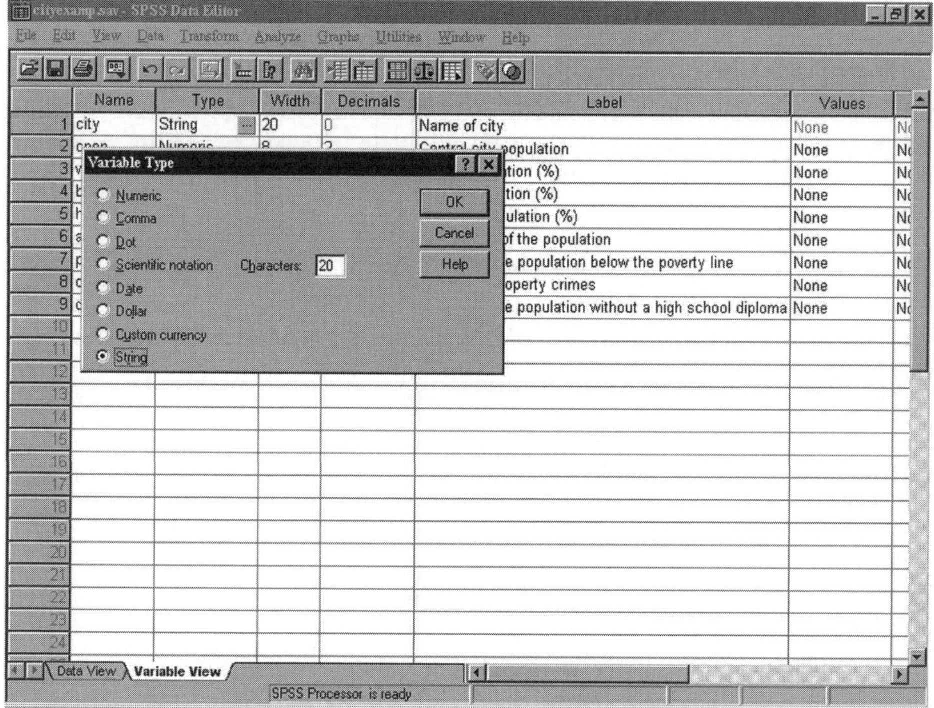

Figure 10-5
Variable Type Dialog Box

Next, you need to increase the width of the **CITY** variable. Click on the cell in the *Width* column and type in the number *20.* This step will allow you to type in the full name of each city when entering data for **CITY.**

If applicable, you may also want to redefine the number of digits to the right of any decimal points. The default number of digits is 2. You do not want to change the default number for this file. For nominal numeric variables, however, the decimal value should be zero. Changing the default value is a simple task. Just click on the cell in the *Decimals* column of the applicable variable and type in the desired number of digits (Figure 10-6).

Figure 10-6
Changing the Decimal Attribute of a Variable

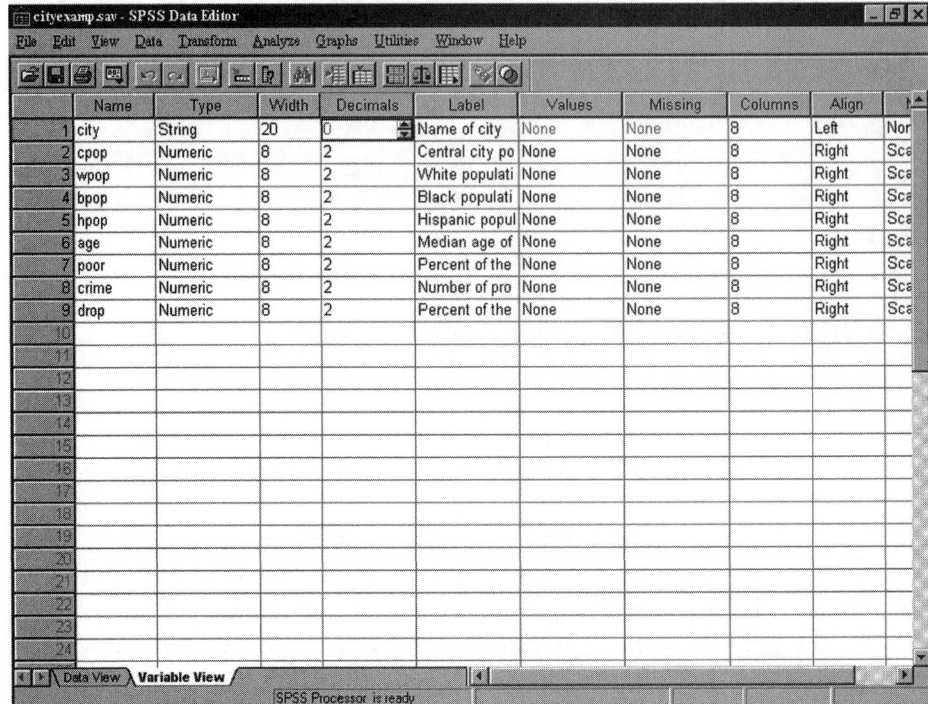

	Name	Type	Width	Decimals	Label	Values	Missing	Columns	Align	M
1	city	String	20	0	Name of city	None	None	8	Left	Nor
2	cpop	Numeric	8	2	Central city po	None	None	8	Right	Sca
3	wpop	Numeric	8	2	White populati	None	None	8	Right	Sca
4	bpop	Numeric	8	2	Black populati	None	None	8	Right	Sca
5	hpop	Numeric	8	2	Hispanic popul	None	None	8	Right	Sca
6	age	Numeric	8	2	Median age of	None	None	8	Right	Sca
7	poor	Numeric	8	2	Percent of the	None	None	8	Right	Sca
8	crime	Numeric	8	2	Number of pro	None	None	8	Right	Sca
9	drop	Numeric	8	2	Percent of the	None	None	8	Right	Sca

If you need to code data, simply click on the cell in the *Values* column and type the appropriate labels in the resulting dialog box (Figure 10-7). For example, 1 = Male and 2 = Female. Repeat these steps for each variable category. (Note: You do not need to assign category values for the city data because each of the variables, except for **CITY,** is a metric variable with natural value labels). After you complete this step, you are ready to enter the data.

10-4 Entering the Data

It is simple to enter data into the SPSSW Data Editor. In fact, entering data in SPSSW is very similar to entering data in any Windows spreadsheet program (like Excel, for example). You will enter data on the Data View tab in the Data Editor window after you have finished defining the variables and their attributes in the Variable View tab.

1. Each row represents a case. In the city data, each case is a city. For a survey, each case is an individual respondent.
2. Each column represents a variable. In the city data, each variable is a characteristic or attribute of the cities included in the file. For example, the second column represents the central city population (**CPOP**).

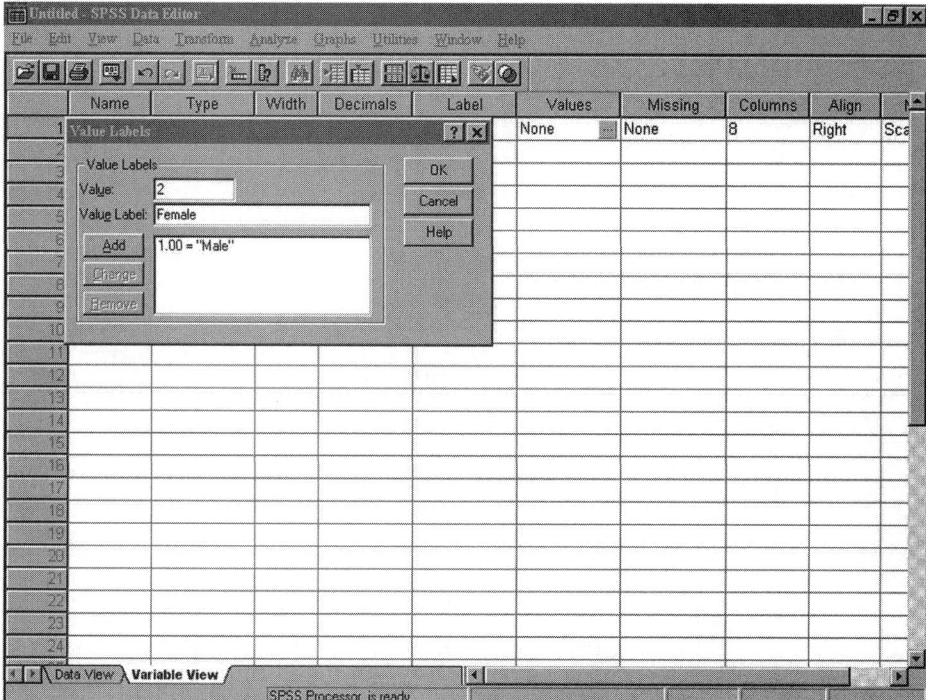

Figure 10-7
Value Labels Dialog Box

3. Each cell contains a single value of a variable for a case. The cell is the intersection of the case and the variable. Cells contain only data values. Unlike spreadsheet programs, however, cells in the Data View cannot contain formulas.
4. The dimensions of a data file are determined by the number of cases and variables. The city data has nine variables (columns) and ten cases (rows). You can enter data in any cell. If you enter data in a cell outside the boundaries, the data rectangle is extended to include any rows and/or columns between that cell and the original boundaries. For numeric variables, blank cells are converted to the system value "Missing." For string (alpha) variables, a blank is considered a valid value. Figure 10-8 depicts the Data Editor window, Data View, before entering the actual city data.

Follow these steps to enter data.

1. Ensure you are working in the Data View tab of the Data Editor window.
2. Begin entering data in row 1, column 1. Click on the cell at the intersection of row 1 (the first case in the data set) and column 1 (the first variable in the data set). Completion of this step will produce Figure 10-9. Notice that there is a thicker border surrounding the cell. The thicker border identifies the *current active cell.*
3. Type in the value of the first case. For the city data, you need to type in "New York." Then press the Enter key on your keyboard.
4. Type in the value of the second case ("Chicago"). Press Enter.
5. Repeat the above steps until you have entered each value for the **CITY** variable.
6. Make the cell at the intersection of row 1 and column 2 the active cell by clicking on the cell.
7. Enter the appropriate value for the variable. In this case, you will be entering the central city population for New York, which is "7322.6". Then press the Enter key on your keyboard.

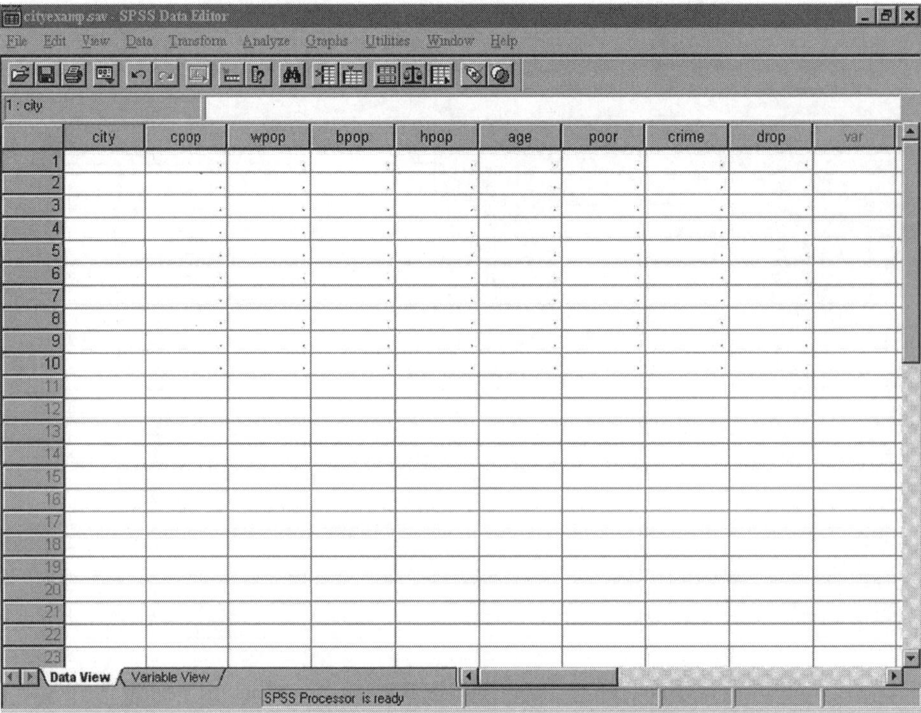

Figure 10-8
Data Editor Window, Data View

8. Type in the value of the second case ("2783.7"). Press Enter.
9. Repeat the above steps until you have entered each value for the **CPOP** variable.
10. Follow the above steps until you have entered data for each case and variable. Completion of the data entry task will produce Figure 10-10.

Figure 10-9
Data Editor Window, Data View, Ready to Enter Data

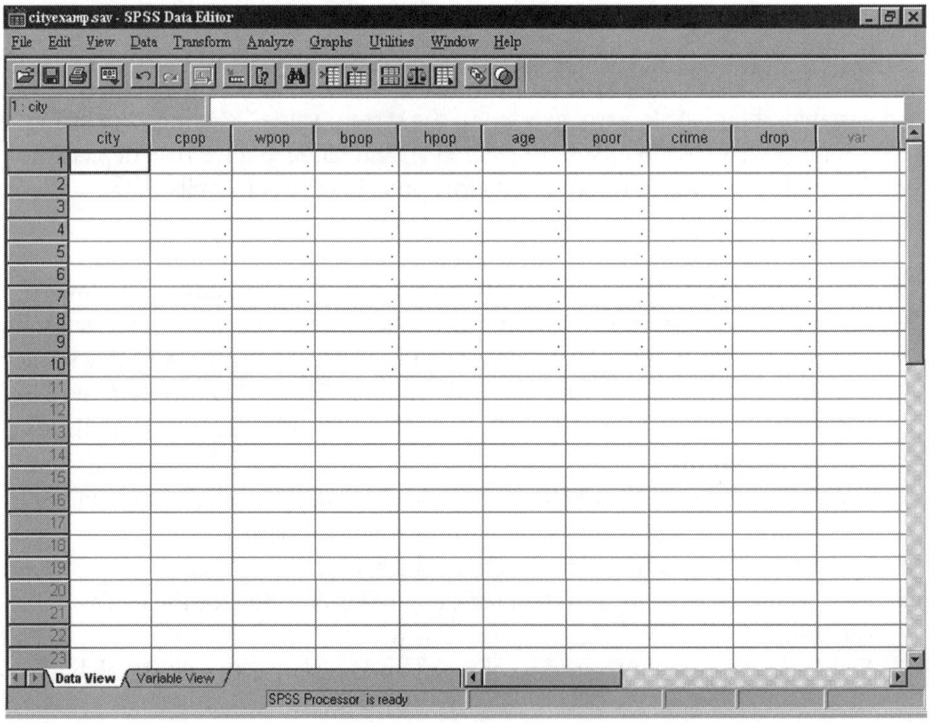

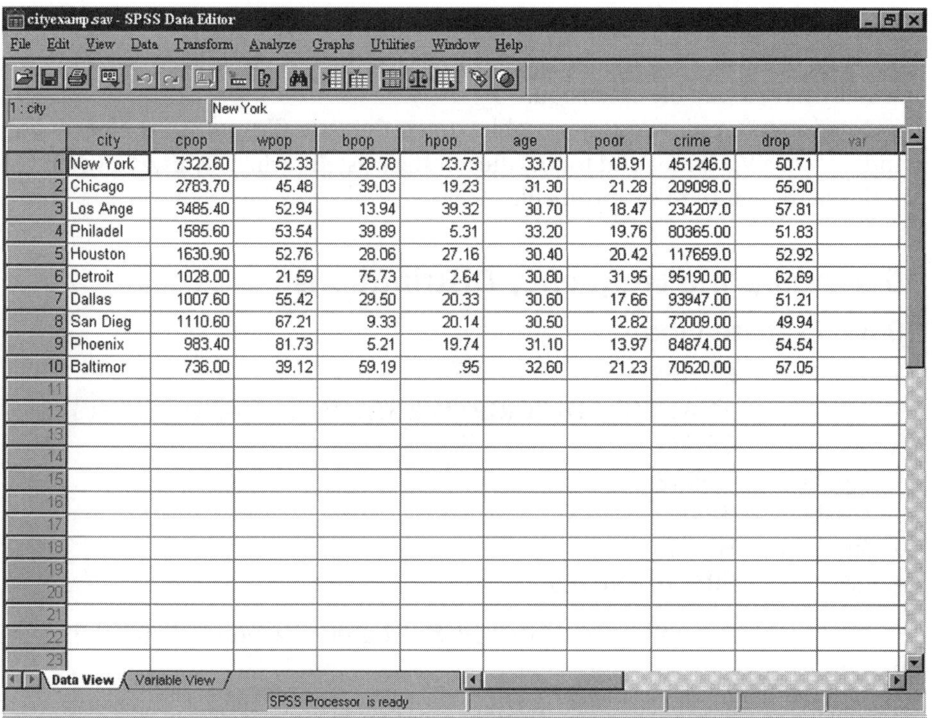

Figure 10-10
Data Entry Example

10-5 Saving the File

After you have finished entering this data set, you need to save your work. Complete the following SPSSW Guide to save your work

→ Task: **File—Save As**

This action produces Figure 10-11. Note that the data will be saved to an external diskette (the *A* drive). If you want to save the data to another drive, just switch to the appropriate drive by clicking the down menu arrow in the *Save As* box.

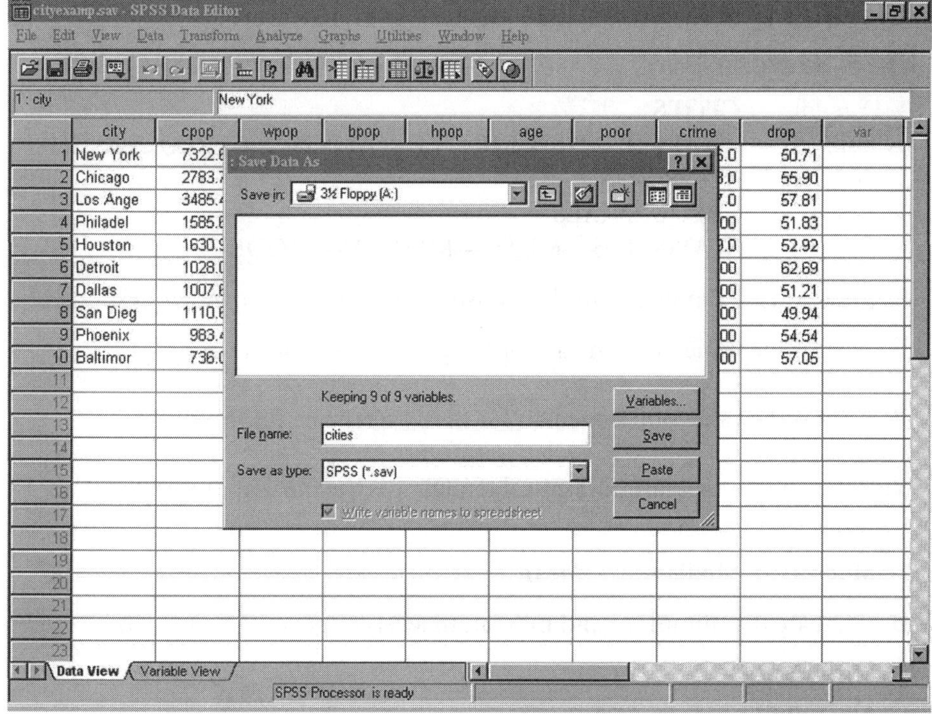

Figure 10-11
Save Data As Dialog Box

Name and save this data set as *cities.* To do this, simply type the word "cities" in the File name box. Click on the Save button to save the file. An SPSSW data file will normally have a *.sav* file extension.

To add more cities and/or variables, open the data file, go to the Data Editor window (Data View tab) and follow the ten steps listed earlier. As always, when you are finished, be sure to save your file.

10-6 Analyzing Frequency Distributions

10-6a Exercise One

→ Data File: **CITIES**
→ Task: **ANALYZE—DESCRIPTIVE STATISTICS—FREQUENCIES**
→ Variable 1: **CPOP**
→ Variable 2: **WPOP**
→ Variable 3: **BPOP**
→ Variable 4: **HPOP**
→ View: **FREQUENCIES**

After you are familiar with the SPSSW output, respond to the following questions.

1. What is the minimum central city population for the cities?

2. What is the maximum white city population (%) for the cities?

3. In what percentage of the cities are there black populations that range from 5.21 percent to 22.54 percent?

4. How many cities have Hispanic populations that range from 2.64 percent to 23.73 percent?

10-7 Analyzing Measures of Central Tendency

10-7a Exercise Two

→ Data File: **CITIES**
→ Task: **ANALYZE—DESCRIPTIVE STATISTICS—FREQUENCIES**
→ Variable 1: **POOR**
→ View 1: **FREQUENCIES**
→ View 2: **STATISTICS—MEAN—MEDIAN—MODE**

After you are familiar with the statistics, answer the following questions.

5. What is the value of the mean for the poverty rate for the cities?

6. What is the value of the median for the poverty rate for the cities?

7. Which of the measures of central tendency is the most appropriate to use? Circle one.

Mode **Median** **Mean**

8. What are the minimum and maximum levels of poverty for the cities?

Minimum ___________
Maximum ___________

10-8 Analyzing Measures of Dispersion

10-8a Exercise Three

→ Data File: **CITIES**
→ Task: **ANALYZE—DESCRIPTIVE STATISTICS—FREQUENCIES**
→ Variable 1: **AGE**
→ Variable 2: **CRIME**
→ View 1: **FREQUENCIES**
→ View 2: **STATISTICS—STD. DEVIATION—MEAN—MEDIAN—MODE**

After you are familiar with the SPSSW output, respond to the following questions.

9. What is the value of the standard deviation for the property crime rate for the cities?

10. What is the value of the standard deviation for the median age for the cities?

11. Which of the measures of central tendency is the most appropriate to use with the property crime rate? Circle one.

Mode **Median** **Mean**

12. Which of the measures of central tendency is the most appropriate to use with the median age level? Circle one.

Mode **Median** **Mean**

13. Succinctly interpret the standard deviation and mean for the property crime rate for the cities.

14. Succinctly interpret the standard deviation and mean for the median age level for the cities.

10-9 Analyzing Graphs

10-9a Exercise Four

→ Data File: **CITIES**
→ Task: **ANALYZE—DESCRIPTIVE STATISTICS—FREQUENCIES**
→ Variable: **DROP**
→ View 1: **STATISTICS—STD. DEVIATION—MEAN—MEDIAN—MODE**
→ View 2: **CHARTS—HISTOGRAM**

Note: Do not display a frequency table for this exercise.

After you are familiar with the SPSSW output, respond to the following questions.

15. Which of the measures of central tendency is the most appropriate to use with the school dropout rate? Circle one.

Mode **Median** **Mean**

16. What is the value of the appropriate measure of central tendency for the school dropout rate?

17. Succinctly interpret the standard deviation and mean for the school dropout rate.

18. How many cities are represented by the third bar in the histogram?

19. How many cities have a dropout rate between 50.0 percent and 53.0 percent?

Chapter Quiz

1. Coding is the process of assigning numbers to all possible responses to all questions or items that make up your database. Coding is necessary when working with ___ data.
   a. nominal
   b. ordinal
   c. metric
   d. Coding is necessary when working with *a* and *b*.
2. Which of the following are important rules to follow when coding data?
   a. Each unit of analysis should fit into one and only one category.
   b. Every response must fit into a category with few responses being classified as "other."
   c. Categories must be specific enough to capture differences while using the smallest possible number of categories.
   d. All of the above are important rules to follow when coding data.
3. The first step to follow when creating a new SPSSW data file is to
   a. define the variable attributes.
   b. display the Variable View in the Data Editor.
   c. define missing values.
   d. assign category value labels.
4. Which of the following rules applies when naming variables in an SPSSW data file?
   a. Variable names must begin with a letter.
   b. Variable names cannot end with a period.
   c. Variable names cannot exceed eight characters.
   d. Blanks and special characters such as ? cannot be used in the variable name.
   e. Each of the above rules applies when naming variables in an SPSSW data file.
5. When entering data into the SPSSW Data Editor
   a. each row represents a variable.
   b. each row represents a case.
   c. each column represents a case.
   d. each cell represents a variable.
6. When entering data into the SPSSW Data Editor
   a. each row represents a variable.
   b. each column represents a case.
   c. each column represents a variable.
   d. each cell represents a variable.
7. The dimensions of an SPSSW data file are determined by the number of
   a. cases.
   b. variables.
   c. The dimensions of an SPSSW data file are determined by the number of cases and variables.
   d. None of the above choices determine the dimensions of an SPSSW data file.
8. The contents of the first cell in an SPSSW data file represent
   a. the first case in the data set.
   b. the first variable in the data set.
   c. the size of the data set.
   d. The contents of the first cell in an SPSSW data file represent the value of the first variable for the first case in the data file.
9. Normally, an SPSSW data file will be saved with the ___ extension.
   a. txt
   b. doc
   c. sav
   d. por
10. Which of the following statements about the SPSSW *cities* data file you created in this exercise are true?
    a. Each variable in the SPSSW *cities* data file is a string variable.
    b. Each variable in the SPSSW *cities* data file is a numeric variable.
    c. Each variable in the SPSSW *cities* data file is a metric variable.
    d. Each variable name has eight or less characters.

Appendix

Data File Descriptions and Sources

Outline

A-1 *Court* Data File: Justices of the U.S. Supreme Court [COURT]

1) **NAME:** Name
2) **YOB:** Year of birth
3) **PID:** Political party
4) **REGION:** Region of residence
5) **LAWSCHOO:** Law school attended
6) **PRESIDEN:** Appointing president
7) **PRIOREXP:** Primary occupational position before appointment
8) **YTO:** Year sworn into office
9) **CHIEF:** Chief Justice?
10) **YLO:** Year left the bench
11) **YOD:** Year of death
12) **DIED?:** Died in office?
13) **APPTAGE:** Age of justice at nomination
14) **YRSSVC:** Years of service on the Court
15) **JUDICIAL:** Judicial experience
16) **PRESPID:** Political party of appointing president
17) **PIDLINK:** Political party of justice and president are the same
18) **JUDYRS:** Actual number of years of judicial experience
19) **YRSSVCCOL:** Years of service on the Court (Note: This is a collapsed variable).
20) **ATTENDLAW:** Did justice attend law school?
21) **NJUDYRS:** Number of years of judicial experience collapsed into 4 categories
22) **RELIGION:** Religious affiliation
23) **GENDER:** Gender of justice
24) **RACE:** Race of justice
25) **IVY:** Did justice attend an Ivy League Law School?
26) **ERA:** Court Era

A-2 *Nations* Data File: Nations of the World [NATIONS]

1) **COUNTRY:** Country name
2) **AREA:** Area in square miles
3) **POPULATI:** Population in 1000s
4) **DENSITY:** Population per square mile
5) **URBAN:** 1995: Percent urban
6) **POPGROWT:** Current annual population growth rate
7) **NETMIGRT:** The balance between the number of persons entering and leaving a country during the year (per 1,000 persons)
8) **BIRTHRAT:** The average annual number of births during a year (per 1,000 population) at mid year; a.k.a. crude birth rate
9) **INFMORT:** Number of infant deaths per 1,000 births
10) **MOMMORTA:** 1990: Maternal mortality rate per 100,000 live births
11) **ABORTLEG:** Is abortion is permitted upon request or for economic or social reasons?
12) **MOMHEALT:** Percent who approve of an abortion when the mother's health is at risk
13) **ABUNWANT:** Percent who approve of an abortion for a married woman who doesn't want another child
14) **DEATHRAT:** The average annual number of deaths during a year (per 1,000 population) at midyear; a.k.a. crude death rate
15) **LIFEEXPC:** Average life expectancy
16) **LIFEXMAL:** Average life expectancy, males
17) **LIFEXFEM:** Average life expectancy, females
18) **SEXRATIO:** Number of females per 100 males

19) **UNDER15:** Percent of population under 15 years of age
20) **OVER64:** Percent of population 65 years old and over
21) **HUMANDEV:** Human Development Index (higher score = more developed)
22) **ECONDEVE:** Level of economic development
23) **QUALLIFE:** Physical Quality of Life Index
24) **DOCTORS:** 1993: Number of physicians per 1,000,000 population
25) **PUBEDUCA:** 1995: Public expenditure on education as percentage of GDP
26) **PUBHEALT:** 1991: Total expenditure on health as percentage of GDP
27) **INEQUALI:** GINI index (Deviation from equal distribution of income or consumption)
28) **GDP:** 1995: Gross Domestic Product in billions of U.S. dollars
29) **REVENUE:** 1995: National government revenue in U.S. dollar equivalents (in millions)
30) **EXPEND:** 1995: National government expenditure in U.S. dollar equivalents (in millions)
31) **IMPORTS:** 1995: Imports in U.S. dollar equivalents (in millions)
32) **EXPORTS:** 1995: Exports in U.S. dollar equivalents (in millions)
33) **TRADE:** 1995: Total trade. Imports plus exports in U.S. dollar equivalents
34) **EXTDEBT:** 1995: External debt in billions of U.S. dollars
35) **INDGROWT:** 1995: Industrial production growth rate
36) **INFLATRT:** 1995: Annual inflation rate
37) **UNEMPLYR:** 1995: Annual unemployment rate
38) **ELECTRIC:** Per capita annual electricity consumption [in kilowatt-hours, 1997]
39) **AGRICULT:** 1995: Percent of GDP [gross domestic product] accounted for by agriculture
40) **INDUSTRY:** 1995: Percent of GDP [gross domestic product] accounted for by industry
41) **SERVICE:** 1995: Percent of GDP [gross domestic product] accounted for by Service sector
42) **HWYVEH:** 1995: Number of highway vehicles (passenger and commercial) (in 1000s)
43) **GREENHOU:** 1991: Per capita carbon dioxide emissions (in metric tons)
44) **LITERACY:** 1995: Literacy rate. Number of people over 15 years of age able to both read and write per 1000 population
45) **RADIO:** 1994: Number of radio receivers (in 1000s)
46) **TELEVISN:** 1994: Number of television sets (in 1000s)
47) **PAPERS:** 1994: Newspapers per 10,000 population
48) **PRIMSEC:** 1990–1995: Primary plus secondary school students (in 1000s)
49) **UNIVRSTY:** 1990–1995: University enrollment (in 1000s)
50) **GRADE5:** 1995: Percent of children who reach grade 5 before quitting
51) **FEMLEGIS:** 1995: Percent of parliamentary seats held by females
52) **GENDEREQ:** 1995: Gender-related Development Index (GDI)
53) **INDPERIO:** Period of independence
54) **NUKES:** Ownership of nuclear weapons
55) **POLRIGHT:** Extent of individual political rights
56) **CIVILLIB:** Extent of individual civil liberties
57) **FREEDOM:** Freedom in the world overall rating as average of political rights and civil liberties
58) **VOTE:** Percentage of eligible voters who voted in the most recent parliamentary election
59) **MULTICUL:** Multiculturalism: odds that any 2 persons will differ in their race, religion, ethnicity (tribe), or language group
60) **CONFLICT:** Index of cultural conflict
61) **DEMOCRAC:** Extent of individual political freedom
62) **FREEECON:** Degree to which the economy is a free market or state regulated

63) **REVOLUTI:** Percent who believe "the entire way our society is organized must be radically changed by revolutionary action"
64) **LEFTIST:** Percent who identify themselves as on the political left
65) **RIGHT:** Percent who identify themselves as on the political right
66) **INTPOLIT:** Percent very or somewhat interested in politics
67) **PETITION:** Percent who have signed a political petition
68) **BOYCOTT:** Percent who have joined in a boycott
69) **DEMONSTR:** Percent who have taken part in a lawful demonstration
70) **TALKPOLI:** Percent who often talk about politics with their friends
71) **DEFENSE$:** Percent total expenditure allocated to defense
72) **MILITARY:** 1996: Size of military in 1000s
73) **MUSLIM:** Percent Muslim
74) **CHRISTI:** Percent Christian
75) **CATHOLIC:** Percent Catholic
76) **HINDU:** Percent Hindu
77) **BUDDHIST:** Percent Buddhist
78) **JEWISH:** Percent Jewish
79) **RELIG:** Percent who described themselves as "a religious person"
80) **GODIMPOR:** Percent saying God is important in their lives
81) **PRAY:** Percent who pray at least sometimes
82) **ASSAULT9:** 1990: Number of assaults per 100,000 population
83) **MURDER90:** 1990: Number of homicides per 100,000 population
84) **RAPE90:** 1990: Rapes per 100,000 population
85) **ROBBERY:** 1990: Robberies per 100,000 population
86) **BURGLARY:** 1990: Burglaries per 100,000 population
87) **THEFT90:** 1990: Thefts per 100,000 population
88) **POLICE:** 1990: Number of police officers per 10,000 population
89) **PRISONER:** Number of prison inmates per 100,000
90) **CAPPUNIS:** Capital punishment
91) **ANTIJEW:** Percent who would not want Jews as neighbors
92) **ANTIFORN:** Percent who would not want foreigners as neighbors
93) **ANTIMUSL:** Percent who would not want Muslims as neighbors
94) **RACISM:** Percent who would not want members of another race as neighbors
95) **ANTIGAY:** Percent who would not want homosexuals as neighbors
96) **UNIONIZE:** Percent who belong to a labor union
97) **POORLAZY:** Percent who said the most important reason that people in their country are poor is "laziness and lack of will power"
98) **INJUSTIC:** Percent who said that people are poor because "there is injustice in our society"
99) **CHEATTAX:** Percent who say it is never justified to cheat on your taxes
100) **SUICIDE:** Suicides per 100,000
101) **SUICIDEN:** Percent who think suicide is never OK
102) **EUTHANAS:** Percent who believe euthanasia is OK (terminating the life of the incurably sick)
103) **AIDS:** 1996: AIDS cases per 100,000 population
104) **DRUGS:** Daily consumption of narcotic drugs, doses per million
105) **SMOKEDOP:** Percent who think it is never OK to use marijuana or hashish
106) **NATLPRID:** Percent who say they are very proud to be (British, American, etc.)
107) **WILLFIGH:** Percent who would fight to defend their country
108) **KIDMANNE:** Percent who think it is important that children learn good manners
109) **REGION:** Region
110) **CDEMOCR:** Extent of democracy collapsed
111) **CMULTICU:** Collapsed multiculuture index
112) **FOAC:** Freedom of association collapsed
113) **CIVLIBC:** Index of civil liberties, collapsed
114) **PETITC:** Petitioning collapsed

115) **EXMARRY:** Percent who say it is OK to carry on an extramarital affair
116) **MEDIA:** Index to measure the extent of the media
117) **RELACTIV:** Scale to measure extent of religious conviction
118) **HAPPY:** Scale to measure extent of satisfaction with one's life
119) **VALUES:** Scale to measure societal values (the higher the score, the greater the opposition to abortion, euthanasia, extramarital affairs)
120) **CGDP:** GDP collapsed into three categories
121) **CTRADE:** Trade collapsed into three categories
122) **CEXTDEBT:** External debt collapsed into three categories
123) **CINDUSTR:** Industry as percentage of GDP collapsed into three categories
124) **CDEFENSE:** Percent allocated to defense collapsed into three categories
125) **CMILITAR:** Size of military collapsed into three categories
126) **CNATPRID:** National pride collapsed into three categories
127) **CWILLFIG:** Percent willing to fight collapsed into three categories
128) **WAR:** Armed conflict engaged in from 1990–1996

A-3 *Presidents* Data File: Presidents of the United States [PRESIDENTS]

1) **NAME:** Last, first name
2) **BIRTHYEA:** Year of birth
3) **AGE1STIN:** Age at (first) inauguration
4) **AGELEAVO:** Age at which President left office (including those that died in office)
5) **PARTY:** Political party affiliation
6) **RELIGION:** Religious affiliation or church preference
7) **DEATHYEA:** Year of death
8) **AGEATDEA:** Age at time of death
9) **YR1STINA:** Year of (first) inauguration
10) **LENGINAS:** Length of (first) inaugural speech by number of words (note: Presidents who were not elected did not give an inaugural speech)
11) **CLEMENCY:** Acts of clemency (pardons, conditional pardons, commutations, remissions)
12) **EXECAGR:** Number of executive agreements signed
13) **TREATIES:** Number of treaties signed
14) **DIPLOMAT:** Number of treaties and executive agreements negotiated
15) **EXECORD:** Number of executive orders
16) **PRESVETO:** Total number of presidential vetoes
17) **VETO:** Number of regular presidential vetoes
18) **POCKET:** Number of pocket vetoes
19) **OVERRIDE:** Number of vetoes overridden
20) **VETOSUCR:** Veto success rate
21) **COURT:** Total number of Supreme Court appointees
22) **CTRULES:** Number of Supreme Court rulings against presidents
23) **LASTYROF:** Last year in office
24) **TIMEINOF:** Time in office (days)
25) **ATTCOLL:** Did they attend college or university?
26) **COLLEGE:** Last college or university attended by name
27) **OCCUPAT:** Previous principal occupation or profession
28) **ZODIAC:** Zodiac birth signs
29) **HOMESTAT:** State of residence at time of election
30) **BIRTHSTA:** State of birth
31) **HEIGHT:** Height in inches
32) **CHILDREN:** Number of children presidents had/have
33) **RANK:** Historical ranking (Siena College Research Institute Survey of U.S. Historians, 1994)

34) **CSPANRAN:** Historical ranking (C-Span Survey of Presidential Leadership 1999)
35) **FEDRANK:** Historical Ranking (Federalist Society)
36) **STATES:** Number of states won in (first) election
37) **UNION:** Number of states in the Union
38) **ELECCOLL:** Percentage of electoral college vote when (first) elected to office [note: Cleveland was elected to two non-consecutive terms]
39) **OPPVOTE:** Number of popular votes for main opponent in (first) election to office
40) **POPVOTE:** Number of popular votes in (first) election to office
41) **OPPECVTE:** Number of electoral votes for main opponent in (first) election to office
42) **TOTEC:** Total electoral college votes available
43) **VOTEPERC:** Percentage of popular vote when (first) elected to the office (note: there was no recorded popular vote until 1824)
44) **VOTEOPP:** Percentage of popular vote for main opponent in (first) election
45) **UNDIVGOV:** Unified or divided government?
46) **PREMILSE:** Previous military service
47) **PREVFEDG:** Previous federal government service
48) **PREVVPSE:** Previous elected service as Vice President (note: Gerald Ford was appointed Vice President)
49) **PREVYRSV:** Years as Vice President
50) **SENATE:** Previous elected service in the U.S. Senate (note: Andrew Johnson served in the Senate after he left office)
51) **HOUSE:** Presidents with previous service in the U.S. House of Representatives (note: John Quincy Adams served in the House after he left office)
52) **GOVERNOR:** Presidents with previous elected service as state governor
53) **MILITARY:** Military service
54) **MILFAME:** Did military contribute to election?
55) **EXORDCOL:** Executive orders collapsed into three categories
56) **TOTVETOC:** Total presidential vetoes collapsed into three categories
57) **CLEMCOL:** Acts of clemency collapsed into three categories
58) **ACTIVE:** Scale to measure presidential activity
59) **COLRANK:** Presidential rankings collapsed into three categories
60) **DIPCOL:** Diplomat collapsed into three categories

A-4 *Senate* Data File: U.S. Senators of the 107th Congress [SENATE]

1) **NAME:** Name
2) **PARTY:** Political party affiliation (note: Sen. James Jeffords of Vermont changed parties from Republican to Independent)
3) **STATE:** State of representation
4) **SEX:** Gender
5) **RELIGION:** Religious affiliation
6) **RACE:** Race
7) **ACU:** American Conservative Union rating
8) **ACUCOLL:** Collapsed ACU ratings
9) **BIRTYR:** Year of birth
10) **MARITAL:** Marital status
11) **OCCUPATN:** Previous principal occupation before taking office
12) **EDUCATIO:** Level of education
13) **TERM:** Number of terms
14) **YRFIRSTE:** Year first elected
15) **VOTPER:** Percentage of vote

16) **ASHCROFT:** Vote in the confirmation of President Bush's nomination of John Ashcroft to be Attorney General
17) **CAMPFIN:** Vote on H.R. 2356 (Bipartisan Campaign Finance Reform Bill) to amend the Federal Election Campaign Act of 1971)
18) **TAXCUT:** Vote on the adoption of the final version of the tax cut bill, reducing taxes by $1.35 trillion
19) **VOTEACT:** Vote on Reid/Specter Amendment No. 2879 to the Equal Protection of Voting Rights Act
20) **OLSON:** Vote in the confirmation of President Bush's nomination of Theodore Bevry Olson to be solicitor general
21) **VIETNAM:** Vote on the extension of nondiscriminatory treatment with respect to the products of the Socialist Republic of Vietnam
22) **PATRIOT:** Vote on H.R. 3162 (USA Patriot Act) to deter and punish terrorist acts in the United States and around the world
23) **BUDGET:** Senators' vVote on the conference report on H. Con. Res. 83, establishing the congressional budget for the United States
24) **VOUCHERS:** Vote on Amendment to the Elementary and Secondary Education Re-authorization bill that would create a demonstration program to allow public school children to use federal funds to transfer to another type of school
25) **BSA:** Vote on BSA Amendment to an education bill proposed by Helms (R-NC). Amendment would allow withholding of funds to public schools that did not make school facilities available to the Boy Scouts of America.

A-5 *States* Data File: United States [STATES]

1) **NAME:** Name
2) **ELAZARPC:** Primary political culture of the state (Elazar)
3) **AREA:** 1990: Land area in square miles
4) **FEDLAND:** 1997: Percent of land owned by federal government
5) **PARKREV:** 1997: Revenue from state parks in 1000s
6) **POP98:** 1998: Total population in 1000s
7) **POPGO98:** Percent change in population from July, 1995 to July, 1998
8) **DENSITY:** 1998: Population per square mile
9) **FEMALE99:** 1999: Percent of population who are female
10) **SEXRATIO:** 1999: Number of males per 100 females
11) **WHITE98:** 1998: Percent white
12) **BLACK98:** 1998: Percent black
13) **LATINO:** 1998 Percent Latino
14) **NATIVE:** 1998: Percent American Indian, Eskimo, or Aleut
15) **ASIAN:** 1998: Percent Asian or Pacific Islander
16) **IMMIGRAN:** 1997: New immigrants admitted per 10,000
17) **FOREIGN:** 1990: Percent foreign born
18) **URBAN90:** 1990: Percent urban
19) **POP18:** Population under 18 years old in 1,000s
20) **MARRIAG9:** 1997: Marriages per 1,000 population
21) **DIVORCE:** 1997: Divorces per 1,000 population
22) **HHPOPCHG:** 1996: Percent change in number of households
23) **HHPOP:** 1996: Persons per household
24) **FEMHEAD:** 1990: Percent of households that are headed by female, no spouse present
25) **BIRTHS:** 1997: Births per 1,000 population
26) **OWNHOME:** 1995: Percent of dwellings owned by occupant
27) **PRISNPOP:** 1990: Percent living in correctional institutions
28) **NURSHMPO:** 1990: Percent living in nursing homes
29) **MENTLPOP:** 1990: Percent living in mental hospitals
30) **JUVINST:** 1990: Percent living in juvenile institutions

31) **EMSHTR:** 1990: Percent living in emergency shelters for homeless
32) **STRPOP:** 1990: Percent living in visible street locations
34) **NORELIG:** 1990: Percent of the population who say they have no religion
35) **JEWISH:** 1990: Percent of the population who give their religious preference as Jewish
36) **CATHOLIC:** 1990: Percent of the population who give their religious preference as Catholic
37) **BAPTIST:** 1990: Percent of the population who give their religious preference as Baptist
38) **CHURCHMB:** 1990: Percent of population belonging to a local church
39) **DEATHS:** 7/1/95–7/1/96: Deaths per 1,000 population
40) **SUICIDES:** 1996: Suicides per 100,000
41) **TEENMAS:** 1997: Percentage of births to mothers under 20 years old
42) **CLDMORT:** 1996: Infant deaths per 1,000 live births
43) **AIDS:** 1995: AIDS/HIV deaths per 100,000
44) **OVRWEIGH:** 1995: Percent of population 18 and over who are overweight
45) **NOHLTHIN:** 1994: Percent of persons without health insurance
46) **VEHICLES:** 1995: Number of registered motor vehicles in 1,000s
47) **CARMILES:** 1993: Annual vehicle miles per capita
48) **SINGLDRI:** 1990: Percent of workers driving alone to work
49) **CARPOOL:** 1990: Percent of workers who carpool
50) **PUBTRNSP:** 1990: Percent who use public transportation to go to work
51) **WALKERS:** 1990: Percent who walk to work
52) **BIKERS:** 1990: Percent who bicycle to work
53) **POOR:** 1998: Percent below poverty level
54) **MEDFAMIN:** 1998: Median family money income in constant 1998 dollars
55) **ELDPOOR:** 1989: Percent of those over 65 who are below poverty level
56) **WELFARE$:** 1995: Maximum monthly welfare grant per family of 3
57) **PUBAID:** 1992: Percent of population receiving public aid (AFDC and SSI)
58) **STAMPS:** 1995: Percent of households receiving food stamps
59) **STAMPCOS:** 1993: Annual cost of food stamp benefits per capita
60) **AFDCCOST:** 1994: Average monthly payment to family on AFDC
61) **AFDCRECS:** 1994: Percent of population receiving aid to families with dependent children (AFDC)
62) **UNEMPLOY:** 1997: Unemployment rate
63) **FUNEMPL:** 1997: Unemployment rate for females
64) **UNEMPL$:** 1997: Average weekly unemployment benefits in dollars
65) **SCHANGLO:** 1994: Percent of those in school who are white
66) **SCHBLACK:** 1994: Percent of those in school who are black
67) **SCHLATIN:** 1994: Percent of those in school who are Hispanic
68) **SCHASIAN:** 1994: Percent of those in school who are Asian
69) **ACHNATIV:** 1994: Percent of those in school who are American Indian
70) **DROPOUT:** 1990: Percent of those 16 to 19 who are not in high school and have not graduated
71) **COLANGLO:** 1990: Percent of whites 25 and over who have college degrees
72) **COLBLACK:** 1990: Percent of blacks 25 and over who have college degrees
73) **COLLATIN:** 1990: Percent of Hispanics 25 and over who have college degrees
74) **COLASIAN:** 1990: Percent of Asians 25 and over who have college degrees
75) **COLNATIV:** 1990: Percent of American Indians 25 and over who have college degrees
76) **PUPIL$:** 1991: Expenditure per pupil in average daily attendance in public elementary and secondary schools in constant 1991–92 dollars
77) **TEACHER$:** 1992: Average annual salary of instructional staff in public elementary and secondary schools in constant 1993–94 dollars
78) **VIOCRIME:** 1997: Violent crimes per 100,000
79) **PROPCRIM:** 1997: Property crimes per 100,000

80) **MURDER:** 1997: Murders per 100,000
81) **RAPES:** 1997: Forcible rapes per 100,000
82) **ROBBERY:** 1997: Robberies per 100,000
83) **ASSAULTS:** 1997: Aggravated assaults per 100,000
84) **BURGLARY:** 1997: Burglaries per 100,000
85) **LARCENY:** 1997: Larceny-thefts per 100,000
86) **CARTHEFT:** 1997: Motor vehicle thefts per 100,000
87) **POLICE#:** 1996: Number of police officers in state and local government per 10,000
88) **EDUC$:** 1997: State government money spent on education per capita
89) **HLTH$:** 1997: State government money spent on health and hospitals per capita
90) **SWELF$:** 1997: State government money spent on public welfare per capita
91) **ROADS$$:** 1997: State government money spent on highways per capita
92) **JAIL$:** 1997: State government money spent on corrections per capita
93) **SSWIDOWS:** 1997: Average monthly social security payment for widows and widowers
94) **SSDISABL:** 1997: Average monthly social security payment to disabled workers
95) **SSRETIRE:** 1997: Average monthly social security payment to retired workers
96) **FEDAID:** 1997: Federal expenditures and aid to state and local governments per capita
97) **BUSH:** 2000: Percent of votes for Bush
98) **GORE:** 2000: Percent of votes for Gore
99) **NADER:** 2000: Percent of votes for Nader
100) **VAPTO:** 2000: Percent of voting age population who voted in presidential election
101) **REGTO:** 2000: Percent of registered voters who voted in presidential election
102) **REGVOTE:** 2000: Percent of voting age population registered to vote (note: North Dakota and Wisconsin don't have preregistration)
103) **MOTORVOT:** 1995–1996: Percent of voter registrations received from motor vehicle offices
104) **LATINOFF:** 1994: Hispanic public officials per 100,000
105) **MEDINAGE:** 1997: Median age of population
106) **REGION:** Census regions
107) **CNORELIG:** Collapsed version of no religious affiliation
108) **CJEWISH:** Collapsed version of Jewish affiliation
109) **CCATHOLI:** Collapsed version of Catholicism
110) **CBAPTIST:** Collapsed version of Baptist affiliation
111) **CEDUC$:** State education spending collapsed into 3 categories
112) **CJAIL$:** State spending on prison collapsed into 3 categories
113) **CWELF$:** State spending on welfare collapsed into 3 categories
114) **CBUSH:** Bush support collapsed into 2 categories
115) **CGORE:** Gore support collapsed into 2 categories
116) **CNADER:** Gore support collapsed into 2 categories
117) **CVOTED:** Percent of voting age population collapsed into 3 categories
118) **CREGVOTE:** Percent of eligible voters registered collapsed into 3 categories
119) **CMOTORVO:** Percent of motor vehicle registrations collapsed into 3 categories

A-6 *Survey* Data File: Selected Variables from the 2000 General Social Survey [SURVEY]

1) **SEX:** Gender
2) **RACE:** Race
3) **EDUCATIO:** Education
4) **MARITAL:** Marital status
5) **PARTY:** Political party affiliation
6) **REGION:** Region of interview

7) **OWNINCOM:** Personal income
8) **FAMINCO:** Total family income
9) **RELIGION:** Religion
10) **POLVIEW:** Perceived political ideology
11) **CHILDREN:** Number of children
12) **BORNUSA:** Were you born in this country?
13) **VOTEIN96**: Did you vote in the 1996 Presidential election?
14) **WHOIN96:** Did you vote for Clinton, Dole, or Perot?
15) **ENVIRON:** Attitude toward spending to improve and protect the environment
16) **HEALTH:** Attitude toward spending to improve and protect the nation's health
17) **CRIME:** Attitude toward spending to halt the rising crime rate
18) **DRUGS:** Attitude toward spending to deal with drug addiction
19) **EDUCATE:** Attitude toward spending to improve the nation's education system
20) **BLACK:** Attitude toward spending to improve the conditions of Blacks
21) **DEFENSE:** Attitude toward spending to improve the military, armaments and defense
22) **FORAID:** Attitude toward spending on foreign aid
23) **WELFARE:** Attitude toward spending on welfare
24) **ATHEISTS:** Should a person who is against all churches and religion be allowed to make a speech in your community?
25) **RACISTSP:** Should a person who believes that Blacks are genetically inferior be allowed to make a speech in your community?
26) **COMSPEAK:** Should an admitted Communist be allowed to make a speech in your community?
27) **MILITSP:** Should a person who advocates doing away with elections and letting the military run the country be allowed to make a speech in your community?
28) **GAYSPEAK:** Should a man who admits that he is a homosexual be allowed to make a speech in your community?
29) **EXECUTE:** Favor or oppose the death penalty for persons convicted of murder?
30) **GUNLAW:** Favor or oppose a law which would require a person to obtain a police permit before he or she could buy a gun?
31) **GRASS:** Legalize marijuana?
32) **SCHPRAY:** Approve of the United States Supreme Court ruling that no state or local government may require the reading of the Lord's Prayer in public schools?
33) **INTERMAR:** Think there should be laws against marriages between (Negroes/Blacks/African-Americans) and whites?
34) **BIBLE1:** What is your interpretation of the Bible?: actual word of God; inspired word of God; or an ancient book of fables?
35) **AFFRMACT:** Favor or oppose preference in hiring and promotion?
36) **BANKS:** Level of confidence in banks and financial institutions
37) **BIGBIZ:** Level of confidence in major companies
38) **RELIGIO:** Level of confidence in organized religion
39) **EDUCATI:** Level of confidence in education
40) **EXECBR:** Level of confidence in the executive branch of the federal government
41) **LABOR:** Level of confidence in organized labor
42) **PRESS:** Level of confidence in the press
43) **MEDICINE:** Level of confidence in medicine
44) **TV:** Level of confidence in television
45) **SUPCOURT:** Level of confidence in the U.S. Supreme Court
46) **SCIENCE:** Level of confidence in the scientific community
47) **CONGRESS:** Level of confidence in Congress
48) **MILITARY:** Level of confidence in the military
49) **ABIRTHDE:** Attitude toward legal abortion if there is a strong chance of serious defect in the baby
50) **ANOWANT:** Attitude toward legal abortion if the woman is married and does not want any more children

51) **AHEALTH:** Attitude toward legal abortion if the woman's own health is seriously endangered by the pregnancy
52) **ALOWAINC:** Attitude toward legal abortion if the family has a very low income and cannot afford any more children
53) **ARAPE:** Attitude toward legal abortion if the woman became pregnant as a result of rape
54) **AASINGLE:** Attitude toward legal abortion if woman is not married and does not want to marry the man
55) **ABORTANY:** Attitude toward legal abortion if the womaen wants it for any reason
56) **TEENBCOK:** Methods of birth control should be available to teenagers?
57) **SEXEDUC:** For or against sex education in the public schools?
58) **PORNLAW:** Attitude toward regulating the distribution of pornography
59) **EUTHANAS:** When a person has a disease that cannot be cured, should doctors be allowed by law to end the patient's life if requested?
60) **SUICILL:** Should a person have the right to end their own life if the person has an incurable disease?
61) **NEWSPAPE:** How often do you read the newspaper?
62) **WATCHTV:** On the average day, about how many hours do you personally watch television?
63) **AIDPOOR:** Government should help poor to people should take care of themselves
64) **AIDMED:** Government should help people with medical costs to people should take care of themselves
65) **AIDBLACK:** Government is obligated to help blacks to there should be no special treatment
66) **MELTPOT:** Should different racial and ethnic groups maintain their distinct cultures or blend in with others?
67) **IMMIGRAN:** Should the number of immigrants from foreign countries who are permitted to come to the United States be increased, remain the same, or be decreased?
68) **ASKFINAN:** Should the government, before giving individuals a secret or top secret clearance, have the right to ask them about their financial history?
69) **ASKCRIME:** Should the government, before giving individuals a secret or top secret clearance, have the right to ask them about possible criminal records?
70) **ASKDRUGS:** Should the government, before giving individuals a secret or top secret clearance, have the right to ask them about their use of drugs?
71) **ASKMENTA:** Should the government, before giving individuals a secret or top secret clearance, have the right to ask them about the state of their mental history?
72) **ASKFORGN:** Should the government, before giving individuals a secret or top secret clearance, have the right to ask them if they have foreign relatives?
73) **ASKDRINK:** Should the government, before giving individuals a secret or top secret clearance, have the right to ask them about their alcohol consumption habits?
74) **ASKSEXOR:** Should the government, before giving individuals a secret or top secret clearance, have the right to ask them about their sexual orientation?
75) **LIETEST:** Should people with secret/top secret clearance be subject to periodic lie detector tests?
76) **TESTDRUG:** Should people with secret/top secret clearance be subject to random drug tests?
77) **USTERROR:** Attitude toward domestic terror actions as compared to 10 years ago
78) **FRTERROR:** Attitude toward threat of foreign terror actions compared to 10 years ago
79) **NUCLRWAR:** Attitude about threat of nuclear war compared to 10 years ago
80) **SPEECH:** Index to measure support of free speech
81) **SPEAKCOL:** Collapsed Index to measure support for free speech
82) **POLPAPR:** In the past two years, have you looked for information about the views or background of a candidate for political office from the newspapers?

83) **POLMAG1:** In the past two years, have you looked for information about the views or background of a candidate for political office in a general news magazine like *Time*?
84) **POLMAG2:** In the past two years, have you looked for information about the views or background of a candidate for political office in a specialityspecialty magazine like *Mother Jones*?
85) **POLTV:** In the past two years, have you looked for information about the views or background of a candidate for political office on the television?
86) **MEDIACON:** Index to measure extent of confidence in the media
87) **MEDIAUSE:** Public's use of the media to obtain political information

A-7 Data File Sources

***Court:* Justices of the U.S. Supreme Court.** Data in this file are from several sources including:

Abraham, Henry J. 1993. *The Judicial Process*, 6th ed. Oxford Press.

Stanley, Harold W., and Richard G. Niemi. 1994. *Vital Statistics on American Politics*, 4th ed. Congressional Quarterly CQ Press.

***Nations:* Data on Nations of the World.** Note: Variables used in this file were adapted from the data archives of Professor Kenneth L. Stewart, Department of Sociology, Angelo State University. The listed sources for his data include:

Freedom House Survey Team Staff. 1995. *Freedom in the World.* Freedom House.

Human Development Report 1993: People's Participation. United Nations Development Program. Oxford University Press.

Human Development Report 1995: Gender and Human Development. 1995. United Nations Development Program. Oxford University Press.

Central Intelligence Agency. 1994. *The World Factbook.*

Famighetti, Robert. 1995. *The World Almanac and Book of Facts.* Mahwah, NJ: World Almanac Books (Funk & Wagnalls).

The World Bank. 1990. *World Development Report 1990.* World Bank Publication (Oxford University Press).

World Values Survey database (for 1990–1993). Institute for Social Research of the University of Michigan. http://www.worldvaluessurvey.org/services/index.html.

***Presidents:* Presidents of the United States.** Several variables used in this file were developed by Martin Zimmermann. The data in this file are from several sources including:

Schmidt, Steffen W., Mack C. Shelley, and Barbara A. Bardes. 1999. *American Government and Politics Today, 1999–2000.* Belmont, CA: Wadsworth.

McKenna, George. 1998. *The Drama of Democracy: American Government and Politics.* 3rd ed. Boston: McGraw Hill.

The White House. The Presidents of the United States. (http://www.whitehouse.gov/history/presidents/).

***Senate:* U.S. Senators of the 107th Congress.** Data in this file are from Internet sites including:

The Library of Congress. Thomas: Legislative Information on the Internet. Website (http://thomas.loc.gov).

C-Span. (http://www.c-span.-org/rollcall).

The United States Senate official web page. (http://www.senate.gov/).

The American Conservative Union. Annual Rating of Congress. (http://www.acuratings.com/).

***States* Data File: United States.** Note: Variables used in this file were adapted from the data archives of Professor Kenneth L. Stewart, Department of Sociology, Angelo State University. The listed sources for his data include:

The U.S. Bureau of the Census. Various years. http://www.census.gov/.

The U.S. Department of Education, The National Center for Education Statistics. Various years.

The Federal Election Committee. *2000 Official Presidential General Election Results.* http://www.fec.gov/pubrec/2000presgeresults.htm.

The U.S. Bureau of the Census. *Statistical Abstract of the United States.* http://www.census.gov/statab/www/

State Rankings 2001. Morgan Quitno Press.

The U.S. Department of Justice. *Uniform Crime Reports* (various years). http://www.fbi.gov/ucr/ucr.htm

Famighetti, Robert. 1995. *The World Almanac and Book of Facts.* Mahwah, NJ: World Almanac (Funk & Wagnalls).

***Survey:* Selected Variables from the 2000 General Social Survey.** Note: Variables used in this file were adapted from the data archives of Professor Kenneth L. Stewart, Department of Sociology, Angelo State University. The source for his data is the 2000 General Social Survey.

Survey conducted by the National Opinion Research Center of the University of Chicago. The principal investigators are James A. Davis and Tom W. Smith. See the following URLs sites for additional information:

http://www.norc.uchicago.edu/projects/gensoc4.asp

http://www.icpsr.umich.edu:8080/GSS/homepage.htm

Suggested Readings

Babbie, Earl, Fred Halley, and Jeanne Zaino. 2000. *Adventures in Social Research: Data Analysis Using SPSS for Windows 95/98.* Thousand Oaks, CA: Pine Forge Press.

Cronk, Brian C. 2002. *How to Use SPSS: A Step-by-Step Guide to Analysis and Interpretation,* 2nd ed. Los Angeles: Pyrczak Publishing.

Green, Samuel B., and Neil J. Salkind. 2003. *Using SPSS for Windows and Macintosh: Analyzing and Understanding Data,* 3rd ed. Upper Saddle River, NJ: Prentice Hall.

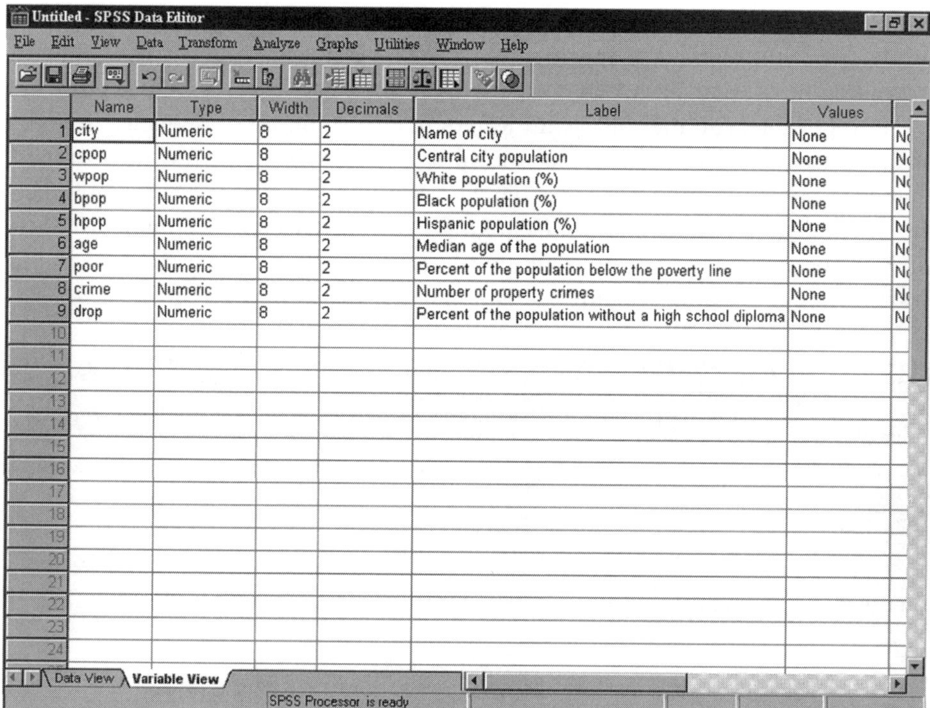

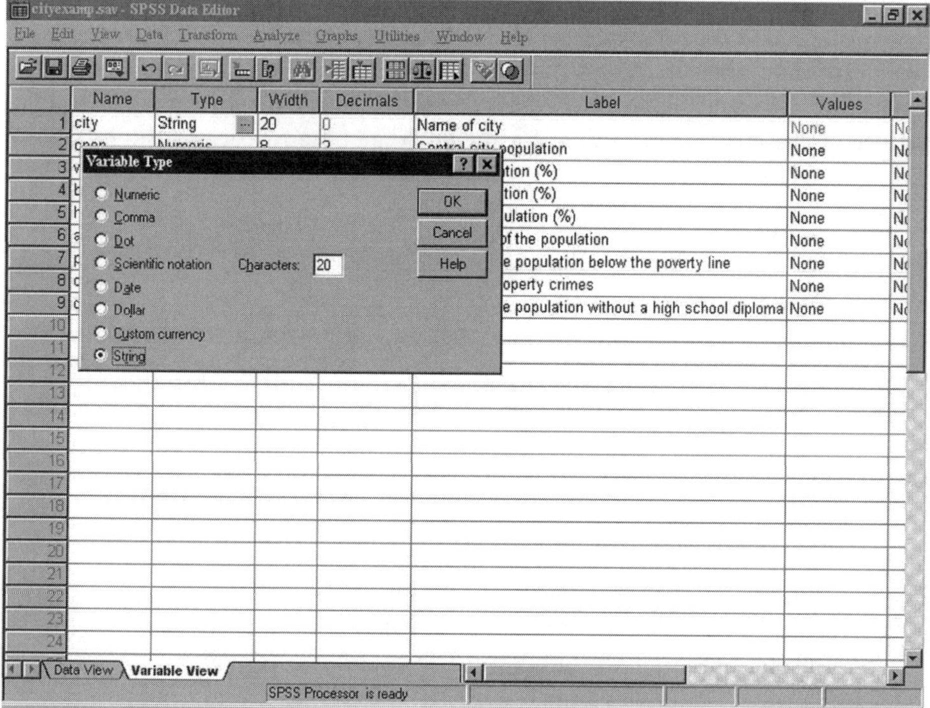

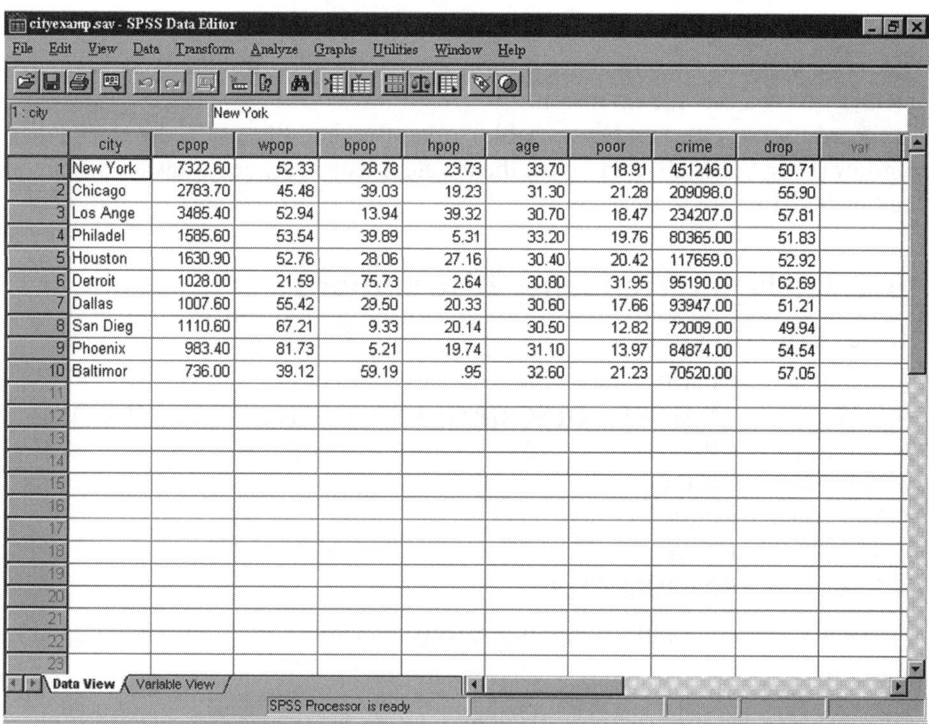

	city	cpop	wpop	bpop	hpop	age	poor	crime	drop
1	New York	7322.60	52.33	28.78	23.73	33.70	18.91	451246.0	50.71
2	Chicago	2783.70	45.48	39.03	19.23	31.30	21.28	209098.0	55.90
3	Los Ange	3485.40	52.94	13.94	39.32	30.70	18.47	234207.0	57.81
4	Philadel	1585.60	53.54	39.89	5.31	33.20	19.76	80365.00	51.83
5	Houston	1630.90	52.76	28.06	27.16	30.40	20.42	117659.0	52.92
6	Detroit	1028.00	21.59	75.73	2.64	30.80	31.95	95190.00	62.69
7	Dallas	1007.60	55.42	29.50	20.33	30.60	17.66	93947.00	51.21
8	San Dieg	1110.60	67.21	9.33	20.14	30.50	12.82	72009.00	49.94
9	Phoenix	983.40	81.73	5.21	19.74	31.10	13.97	84874.00	54.54
10	Baltimor	736.00	39.12	59.19	.95	32.60	21.23	70520.00	57.05

Figure 10-10
Data Entry Example

10-5 Saving the File

After you have finished entering this data set, you need to save your work. Complete the following SPSSW Guide to save your work

→ Task: **File—Save As**

This action produces Figure 10-11. Note that the data will be saved to an external diskette (the *A* drive). If you want to save the data to another drive, just switch to the appropriate drive by clicking the down menu arrow in the *Save As* box.

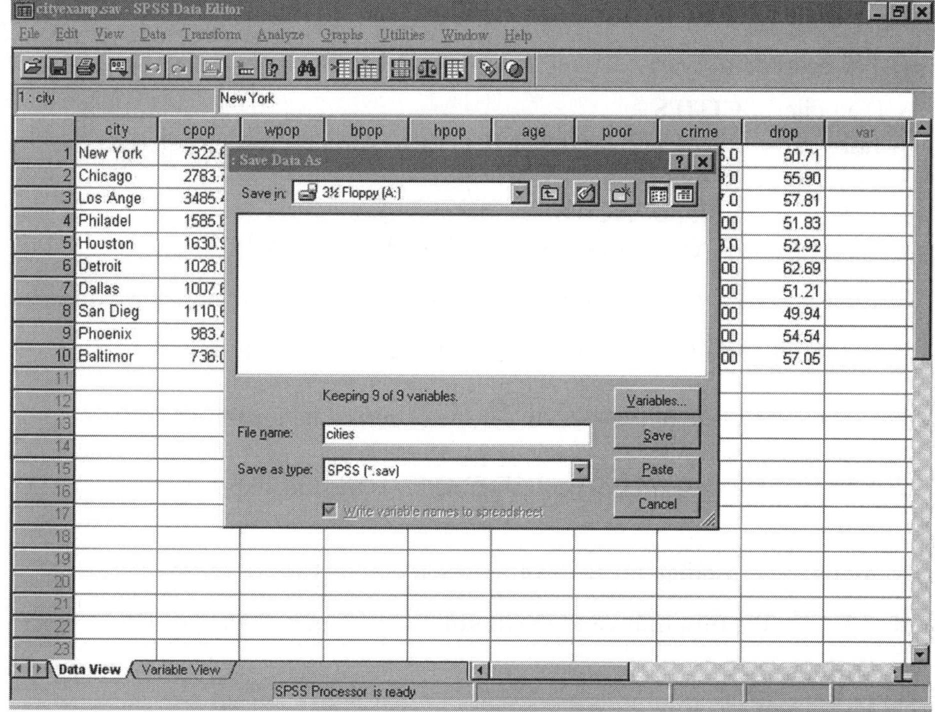

Figure 10-11
Save Data As Dialog Box

Appendix

Appendix

Data File Descriptions and Sources

Outline